POSITIVE LEADERSHIP IN PROJECT MANAGEMENT

A Practical Guide to
Enhancing Individual, Team
and Organizational Performance

FRANK P. SALADIS, PMP

IIL PUBLISHING, NEW YORK

Copyright © 2013 by International Institute for Learning, Inc.

All rights reserved. No portion of this book may be reproduced, stored in a retrieval system, or transmitted in any form or by any means—electronic, mechanical, photocopying, recording, scanning, including the right of reproduction in whole or in part in any form, except for brief quotations in critical reviews or articles, without the prior written permission of the publisher. For information, contact the publisher.

The information in this book is distributed without warranty. Although every precaution has been taken in the preparation of this book, neither the author nor the publisher shall have any liability with respect to any loss or damage caused in any manner by the information contained in this book.

IIL Publishing, New York titles may be purchased in bulk at a discount for educational, business, fund-raising, or sales promotional use. For information, please email Vanessa.Innes@iil.com or call (212) 515-5177.

Published by IIL Publishing, New York, a division of International Institute for Learning, Inc., 110 East 59th Street, 31st Floor, New York, NY 10022

www.iil.com

Publisher: Judith W. Umlas
Text Design: Maria Scharf Design
based on layout by Tony Meisel
Cover Design: Aramazt Kalayjian, FFm, GDE

Library of Congress Cataloging-in-Publication Data available.

ISBN 978-0-9708276-6-1

Printed in the United States of America

Author's Note

The perception of leadership and what it means to be a great leader has changed significantly in the last few years. Many of those who were thought to be true and effective leaders have failed their organizations and their constituents in the pursuit of their own personal gain. It is essential for this trend to reverse.

In the project management environment capable leaders are needed to motivate teams, achieve project success and enhance their organization's brand and abilities. Leaders must encourage collaboration between functional entities, create a supportive environment and instill a sense of positive and authentic leadership throughout the organization. Leaders must establish a strong connection with their project teams and with the many organizational interfaces engaged in managing projects and programs. Perhaps, with all of the challenges we face today, project managers now have a great call to action and an opportunity to demonstrate to the business world what is meant by true and positive leadership.

—*Frank P. Saladis, PMP*

Dedication

This book is dedicated to the many leaders I have met and worked with who have trusted me, encouraged me, supported me, helped me overcome life's challenges and helped me understand the true nature of leadership.

Acknowledgments

My sincere thanks to my many mentors and friends in project management for their continued support, especially: Dan Ono, who opened the door of project management to me, my dear friend Lyn Holly, Dr. Harold Kerzner; Patricia Higgins; Jerry Brightman, who helped me understand that leadership starts from within, Greg Balestrero, a true inspirational leader and professional, Jim Schneidmuller; Ray Ju; the PMI® NYC Chapter Board of Directors, with special thanks to Andrew Gerson for his continued valuable feedback and support; the PMI® Global Operations Center, especially Brantlee Underhill and Anne Jenneme; the PMI® Leadership Institute Masters Class Alumni; Gary Heerkens, who inspires me to find new opportunities; John Schmitt; Lori Milhaven, a true friend; E. LaVerne Johnson, who saw in me a potential to grow; Judy Umlas, who continually tests my creativity; Wayne Dix, who inspires me to achieve new levels of knowledge; and most importantly, my wife Barbara who, in my opinion, is a natural born project manager and has the ability and drive to keep me on task!

Table of Contents

FOREWORD xi

AN INTRODUCTION xv

1. Success is No Reason to Stop Seeking Success 1
2. Leading Project Managers and Teams to Higher Levels of Competency and Effectiveness 9
3. The Art of Meeting Leadership 19
4. Business Savvy and the Project Manager 25
5. Value, Success and Twelve Factors for Effective Project Leadership 35
6. Redefining Project Leadership 49
7. Lead Like Everyone's Watching 59
8. Establishing the Roles of the Project Team 65
9. Leadership Lessons Learned 73
10. How 'Ya Doin'? 81
11. What Project Managers Already Know 89
12. Leadership Lessons from the Future 97
13. Oyakudachi 105
14. Assessing Leadership 111
15. The Importance of Creativity in the Project Team 117
16. The Future's So Bright, We Gotta Wear Shades 123
17. Retaining Your Key Team Members 131
18. Managing Your Leadership Role 139
19. Creating Your Personal Leadership Checklist 145

20. The Importance of Connective Leadership	153
21. In Pursuit of Wow! Leadership	163
22. When Leaders Need Leadership	169
23. Encouraging Innovation	173
24. Common Sense Project Leadership	179
25. Connecting with Executives	185
26. Elongate Your Dendrites	191
27. Achieving Extraordinary Results: The Leadership Formula	199
28. Where Have All the Leaders Gone?	205
29. The Leader and Conflict Management	211
30. The Art of Managing Expectations	219
31. Creating the Energy to Lead	227
32. Lessons Learned from the Last Lecture	233
FINAL THOUGHTS	239
NOTES	241
INDEX	251
ABOUT IIL	260

Foreword

In the early years of project management, engineers were appointed as project managers primarily because the customers were demanding project leaders that possessed a true command of technology, not just an understanding of technology. The majority of these engineer-type project managers had never taken any coursework on leadership or interpersonal skills. Even if they had taken such courses, the material would most likely have focused on traditional line management leadership, stressing superior-subordinate relationships, rather than project-focused leadership. Project management leadership was basically viewed as management of technology.

Executives appointed project managers based upon their technical knowledge and ability to handle technical decision-making. During the interview process for prospective project managers, emphasis was placed on the ability to manage scope, time and cost, rather than on interpersonal skills and human relations.

During project closure or termination, when a debriefing session was held for a project that failed or missed milestones, the blame was usually placed on poor planning, estimating, scheduling and control. In other words, it was viewed as a *quantitative failure*. But some projects were failing because of behavioral considerations, namely:

- Poor morale
- No employee commitment
- No functional unit commitment
- Poor productivity
- Poor human relations
- Ineffective real project leadership

Today, people who are involved in the selection of project managers, especially executive managers and project sponsors, have realized that in many cases, project failure is directly linked to human behavioral issues and that these failures are, for the most part, attributed to a poor understanding of effective project leadership.

Traditional leadership focuses heavily on a manager–subordinate relationship, specifically focusing on how the manager should provide leadership to subordinates. When discussing traditional leadership, three very important assumptions are generally made:

- The line or functional manager (also known as the boss or supervisor) has authority over the worker/performer.
- The line manager has wage and salary responsibility for the worker.
- The line manager has sufficient time to get to know the worker.

However, in the project environment, these assumptions may not be valid. The following elements are characteristic of a project environment, which help us to better understand the complexities of project leadership:

- Employees are assigned to the project team by their respective line or functional managers, and usually remain as direct reports during the execution of the project.
- The employees may be working on several projects concurrently, and therefore must adapt to the leadership styles of several project managers, as well as their line manager.
- Project managers may request specific people for their project, but the final decision on the assignment usually rests with the line manager.
- The project manager does not possess the authority to have people removed from a project team, unless the line manager supports the removal.
- The duration of the team member's assignment to the project team may be so short that the project manager never gets to know the worker.
- The team member resides in his or her functional area and

- The project manager may not have a great deal of contact with the team members outside of project team meetings.
- The project manager generally has limited or no responsibility for wage and salary administration for team members.
- The employees assigned to the team are often at higher pay grade and salary levels than the project manager.
- The project manager may have limited or no control over rewards such as salary, bonus, overtime and future work assignments.
- The project manager may possess some degree of assumed authority, but may have very little legitimate authority, regardless of what appears in the project charter. Project management is, very often, leadership without authority.
- Line managers can manage with just one leadership style because of their wage, salary administration responsibility and job description, whereas project managers may need to develop and utilize different leadership styles for each person assigned to the project team and the many other stakeholders that may be involved in the project.
- The project manager's leadership style may need to change over the life cycle of the project.

Given all of these complexities, it should be no surprise to anyone as to how difficult it is to provide effective leadership when managing a project team. Despite the vast quantity of research on traditional leadership, theorists have yet to come up with a perfect model that can be universally applied. The fundamental mechanics of project management are fairly easy to learn and apply, but project leadership, which involves dealing with a variety of people, personalities, communications styles and cultures can be difficult to master.

Football coaches in the National Football League (NFL) understand the mechanics of football. Yet few have achieved the fame of legendary Green Bay Packers' coach, Vince Lombardi. Lombardi had an exceptional ability to maximize the output of each of his players. He applied the principles of leadership to each team member, one-on-one, and felt a sense of true reward and pride when the players performed at their personal best. This was leadership at its finest and something that project managers should strive for.

Frank's manuscript, *Positive Leadership in Project Management*, is a comprehensive, state-of-the-art book that focuses on real-world techniques that work! He moves away from the typical project management text that has a preoccupation with planning and scheduling, and focuses on people and performance. The book says little about traditional leadership techniques and theories that most practitioners find inappropriate, and instead focuses on the relationships between project leadership, people and success.

This book is a collection of critical success factors, key performance indicators and lessons learned based upon Frank's decades of experience in project management and the wisdom of many well-known thought leaders. The book helps us determine the true characteristics of an effective project leader under a variety of real world situations.

In my opinion, *Positive Leadership in Project Management* is a must-read for anyone who has a desire to improve his or her project leadership ability on a long-term basis. Anyone can be successful when assigned to manage a single project by using formal authority, brute force and a big stick. These tactics have been commonly used to meet project objectives and there are many people who continue to use them. But to be truly successful on a continuous basis, the key is to connect with people and inspire each person on every project team to attain his or her personal best and to develop their own leadership skills. A leader who enables others to lead is one who will clearly make a difference in his or her organization. I believe that if you follow the recommendations provided in this text, you will be taking a great step forward in the continuing journey known as leadership.

Harold Kerzner, Ph.D.
Senior Executive Director for Project Management
International Institute for Learning, Inc.

An Introduction

Despite the effort placed on planning, coordinating and integrating the many components of a project, the project manager's typical day is filled with challenge - an unending stream of e-mail, deadline issues, some frustrating events (and people), conflicting view points from stakeholders and some successes and victories. At the end of the day, it is sometimes difficult to remember what actually happened and what was accomplished. The activities of the day are often blurred by the thoughts associated with the preparations and steps taken to begin another set of adventures just waiting for their chance to occur with the start of the next morning.

Dealing with this intense mode of operation on a regular basis places a very heavy demand on the abilities of a project manager and there is a real need to find some way to balance the competing elements that go along with the job. This balance extends to one's personal and family life also. The question then becomes "How can we (as project managers) find that balance?" In the book, *First Things First* by Roger A. Merrill and Stephen Covey, a suggestion is offered: "Know the direction in which you intend to go and your goals on a personal and professional level."[1] In other words, a clear sense of direction should be defined for your personal life as well as your chosen profession. To a practicing project manager, that advice should be familiar. In fact, it is essential for project success. Without direction and a set of objectives, how will we ever know where we are going? How can we lead a team if we do not have goals to guide them? There is no question that goals and purpose must be defined, refined and communicated. Without this clarity, we cannot effectively lead our teams, our organization or our own lives. This is where leadership becomes a critical factor.

The project manager is clearly in a leadership role and for us to succeed as project managers, we must achieve balance for ourselves and our own lives. We must then use that balance to heighten our ability to influence and lead our project teams and those who depend on us for guidance, support, direction and motivation.

This book is kind of like a balancing tool for project managers. I consider it to be like the pole used by a tightrope walker to maintain a steady and even approach as he travels from one side to the other. Balance is needed to manage the stressful and risky situations often encountered by project managers.

Considering the importance of balancing the personal life and the business life of the project manager, a book focused on project leadership from a practical perspective is needed. This book is a collection of suggestions, ideas and techniques that will be a helpful addition to the many other resources used for effectively managing and balancing the project manager's daily life. Through the author's personal experience, references to many different articles and sources of information developed by well-known and respected experts in the topic of leadership and through tools, techniques and interesting stories, the project leader will find a kind of "leadership body of knowledge" embedded in the pages.

The main focus of this book is *project leadership* and specifically *Positive Leadership*. There are many styles of leadership in the business world and in the project environment. Without much effort, a long list of commonly recognized leadership characteristics can be developed by any group or team of people. The key is to learn about true, authentic and value-adding leadership and determine what works best for each of us. We need to know which key items from the vast knowledge stores of leadership we should tap into and develop, which will help us achieve balance as managers and leaders.

Begin to balance the demands of the project management profession by reading each chapter with purpose, looking for a few gems of wisdom offered by the experts. Discover your own gems that may be hidden in a story or found between the lines. Use the information to identify new ways to lead your team and your life. Then embark upon your own (continuing) journey towards Positive Leadership with this book and the advice of the many leaders referenced within. Consider this book, and the resources offered on each page, as your personal leadership partners.

Leadership in Project Management — Getting Started

During a class about project management fundamentals that I was recently facilitating, the subject of *Communications Management* became the focus of discussion. We, as project managers, know the importance of effective communication as we manage the project life cycle, especially when working with key stakeholders. However, we may not realize how important communication is to *People Success*. During the class discussion, one participant offered this observation about managers and communication:

> "The problem with management is that they spend more time listening to what they are about to say, than what is being said to them."

This is an interesting observation. I don't believe that this situation is limited exclusively to managers. Everyone has been guilty of this particular behavior at one time or another. If we are not skilled listeners, how can we become great leaders? If we do not listen to the suggestions and ideas of others and respect their points of view, even if we don't agree with their perspectives, how can we grow?

Leadership is a combination of many qualities and the skill of listening is only one component of a much larger and complex skill set. The critical issue here is that if we are not listening to those around us, how will we know what is actually going on in areas that we are not directly involved in or cannot see? How will we know what issues are most important from our team members' perspective? How will we know if our actions are appropriate if we don't have the facts we need? How will we obtain the information that is necessary prior to making a decision? If we are not skilled listeners, how will we know how much of what we missed was truly important? On several occasions during classes and discussions, I've asked project managers from different industries to describe the characteristics of a leader. Generally, a variety of characteristics surface, but at or near the top of the list from every group responding to this simple exercise is *effective communicator*.

There is no question, at least from my point of view, that a major factor in effective and successful communication is the art of **LISTENING**. Any discussion about communications will generally conclude that the truly effective leader listens carefully to his or her teams, employees, families and associates and makes decisions or takes action based on what has been heard, processed and understood. People know it when someone is listening with sincerity and they do appreciate it. Conversely, failure to listen can be severely damaging to any relationship and it can be the root cause of many unfortunate and preventable conflicts.

Connecting communications to Positive Leadership basically comes down to *active listening*. The key components of *active listening* are:

ACTIVE LISTENING

L	=	**Like to listen**	Make listening an enjoyable part of your day.
I	=	**Inspire openness**	Show your interest for honest, sincere comments.
S	=	**Summarize**	Take the time to review what has been discussed.
T	=	**Tame emotions**	Remain focused on the issue and facts.
E	=	**Eliminate hasty decisions**	Don't jump to conclusions or solutions.
N	=	**NEED to listen**	You don't know everything. Obtain information.
I	=	**Ignore distractions**	Give the speaker your undivided attention.
N	=	**Never interrupt**	Wait for the appropriate time to respond.
G	=	**Generate conclusions**	Review what has been discussed.

I don't know the source of this brief, but very useful, gem of communications wisdom but I carry it with me wherever I am speaking and share it with as many people as possible. Of course, being a good listener is not the only skill required to become a great leader, but it certainly is important and worth the effort to master.

The Ever Increasing Knowledge Bank of Leadership

Considering the vast amount of information available, I can't claim this book is filled with new revelations about leadership or that it contains information that has never been shared before, but it is my sincere desire for you to find value in the pages of this book. There are many sources of information about leadership, and many truly effective leaders have shared their knowledge through articles, books and presentations. I have been, and continue to be, inspired by numerous leadership experts such as John C. Maxwell, General Colin Powell and Kevin Cashman. We need more of their type. We need new leaders who will inspire others to greatness. Considering the many resources and amount of knowledge that has been published about leadership, I have attempted to take what I believe to be some of the most useful information available, from a large collection of material developed by knowledgeable and inspiring people, to create a quick reference that will enhance the personal value of the practicing project manager and enrich the experience of leading a project team.

In each chapter you will find a tool called "Your Personal Leadership Action Register," in which you will be encouraged to make a note of insights, key learning points, personal recommendations, areas for review, books to read, actions to take, people to talk to and topics of interest you would like to research. Utilizing it fully can dramatically improve your chances of success at Positive Leadership in project management.

I believe that people who have been assigned roles as project managers have been given a leadership responsibility, regardless of project size or complexity and Positive Leadership is the key to successful teams and successful projects.

Consider your role as a project manager. It is much more than simply making sure that project tasks are completed. The role involves commitment, the ability to influence, personal integrity and the ability to create value. Every project assignment is an opportunity to enhance your leadership skills. Learn from each experience and continue to raise your personal bar of leadership effectiveness.

1 Success is No Reason to Stop Seeking Success

> "Becoming a leader is a lot like successfully investing in the stock market. If your hope is to make a fortune in one day you're not going to be successful."
> – John C. Maxwell

> "Nothing in your past guarantees that you will continue growing toward your potential in the future."
> – John C. Maxwell

A quote that caught my attention, from an article in *Fast Company* magazine is: "We get stupid when we start succeeding."[1] Success is a wonderful thing and we should all strive for it in our personal lives and during every project assignment. This quote does, however, bring to mind something that we have all experienced during periods in which we were most successful: a feeling of safety, security and maybe even invincibility. Success brings upon us a comfortable feeling that we would like to have surrounding us for as long as possible. That same feeling can also cause project managers and project team members to become complacent and to temporarily lose sight of other important issues and problems. This feeling of extreme confidence can cause us to subconsciously reduce our work effort and intensity and pay less attention to important details. That, in turn, can result in a weakening of preparedness.

It is our job as project managers to deliver a successfully completed project. Success may be defined in many ways but let's just say we are seeking a satisfied customer and a proud project team. This is often far easier said than done and when the project is delivered to the sponsor or client and fully meets expectations, there should be time set aside for celebration and recognition. But along with celebrations, attention should be given to lessons learned and some thought about new assignments and what events may be in store for us in the near future. Project managers are either working on highly complex projects that span several years and impact several organizations and cross multiple continents, or they are working on multiple projects with durations of a few weeks to a few months. It is important to maintain an awareness of factors that can turn a potential celebration of success into a project management nightmare.

Keep Your Back to the Wall

The article in *Fast Company* magazine also mentions the need to "keep your back to the wall."[2] This means that some pressure should be felt by the team or the organization, even if things appear to be going well. Instead of working in an environment where the team expects to drive hard for a period of time, expecting to see a slump at the end of the project where everyone can relax and bask in the glory, there should be a sense of preparedness for the next potential project or significant event. This is not to suggest that teams should not be rewarded for their excellent work or that they should be expected to operate at 110 percent efficiency and productivity all of the time. Sufficient time should be planned to allow the team to have a chance to recharge while observing the fruits of their efforts. Failure to recognize, reward and rest can create significant human resource-related problems later on.

The issue or challenge facing project leaders is the need to make sure that after every success, the momentum of the success continues to fuel the team. In many cases a feeling of complacency, even superiority, overtakes a project team or an organization after a big "win." At that point, the team may lose its focus on the higher level objectives of the organization. This is where the team may become most vulnerable to unseen risk factors and threats to the organization. Many championship teams go from the top spot in one season to the last spot in the next season. One major reason is the loss of the edge that was created by "slacking off" or spending too much time congratulating themselves and convincing themselves of their superiority and invincibility.

The leader must balance the need to recognize and celebrate success with the need to keep the team moving forward to the next level of achievement.

This can be a challenge, but it is far better to enjoy a continuous series of small successes than one huge success followed by long periods of inactivity and disappointment. The leader provides the motivational fuel needed to continue the drive to new successes. The drive is punctuated along the way with recognition pit stops, points in time where accomplishments are noted, teams are thanked, refueling of energy and commitment takes place and words of encouragement are provided to help get to the next finish line. It is also important to keep the customer in mind at all times. The *Fast Company* magazine article suggests that you should "remember the driver."[3] The driver refers to the customer or client that buys and uses the products or services. Success is largely measured by customer satisfaction or to state it another way, customer satisfaction defines success. When a customer is satisfied it is cause for celebration, but it is also a time to consider exactly what occurred to bring about this success. Take the time, along with rewards and recognition, to review lessons learned, obtain feedback and encourage the team to do more of what it took to achieve the success.

One more key point that requires some attention is the need to clearly understand how success is defined by each project stakeholder. If customer satisfaction defines success, we need to know exactly what it will take to achieve customer satisfaction. On time, within scope and within budget are factors commonly used to define success but there is much more involved. We also have a need to know how project team members and other stakeholders perceive success. Make sure your entire team understands that they are all in the project together, working towards a mutually- agreed -upon set of goals and objectives. It would be difficult to claim success if a project team completes a project based on the objectives, but is unwilling to work with the project manager or anyone on the team again. The objectives may have been met but the relationships have been destroyed. Not exactly a success story. This is clearly an indication of weak or ineffective leadership.

Create a Vision

A common vision gets your team started. It is a basic element of project management. The team as a cohesive unit should be able to clearly see where they are going. Make sure you have communicated the objectives and your personal vision of the project and why you are enthusiastic about the opportunity. Next, the leader must find a way to energize the team and create a unified desire to step up to the tasks that await them. An energized team, fueled by Positive Leadership, will find a way to overcome any obstacle. As a father of four girls, all of whom were involved in some type of sports, I have seen the results of teams led by great leaders and those led by poor leaders. Believe me, I prefer the effect and the atmosphere created by the great leader. The unity of the team is the key to achieving objectives and a unified team focuses on success. Continued success is the payoff of Positive Leadership on a sports team, or any team, including a project team.

A Quick Reference List of Measurements of Success

In the project management profession, when the question is asked: "How is project success determined?" The common response is what every project manager has been taught for years – "on time, within budget and within specifications or scope." Those factors may be important, but are only a few of the many ways in which success can be measured. Some additional metrics or methods that may be used to determine project success include:
- organizational revenue growth
- earnings per share

- efficiency in the use of organizational resources
- retention of customers
- add-on business
- team member satisfaction—willingness of the team members to continue working as a team on other projects
- increased market share
- customer satisfaction—there are many factors associated with customer satisfaction: high quality, on time performance, cost control, mean time to repair, responsiveness, availability, ease of doing business with and reliability to name a few
- safety in the use of the product
- reduction in staff turnover—minimal loss of key employees
- reduction in the number /frequency of change requests
- reduced average time to respond to problems—satisfactory help desk metrics
- reduced number of defects identified and repaired
- the product of the implementation is actually being used by the end users or customer
- transparency—the project wasn't noticed by other employees in the organization. It didn't disrupt operations or make the front page of the local news. (No news may be good news for some projects.)
- visible senior leadership involvement and communication personal satisfaction and perceived self-value—from the project manager perspective and the team member perspective

A project's success is also determined by a feeling of accomplishment and personal value when the job is completed. The entire team should feel a sense of fulfillment and pride.

Consider how you personally measure project success. What other success metrics can you add to this list? Regardless of how you measure success, the last item on my list (personal satisfaction and perceived self-value) should hold the greatest level of importance. Success means that you and your team have experienced some high level of self-actualization and personal value from the work you have completed. This is a great feeling and is something you want to continue experiencing. It is important to maintain that sense of accomplishment, so keep looking down the road toward the horizon and imagine the next great thing you will do. Take a moment to reflect on your current success and then set your sights forward. Your next success is just ahead, so drive on!

The remaining chapters of this book will build upon on the theme of, or the journey to, Positive Leadership. My intent is to provide project managers with a view of leadership that makes sense in the project environment and to clearly show the connection between successful project management, leadership, team well-being, customer satisfaction, personal value and organizational success.

Your Personal Leadership Action Register

Use the ideas and suggestions in this book to develop a plan for your own personal growth as a leader. Each chapter contains many references and sources of information that will assist you on your leadership journey. Use these references and any personal notes and observations you document to assist you in designing a plan that will achieve your leadership goals. Keep in mind that once you have achieved your defined goals, you need to set new goals and continue your professional development. You are on a leadership journey. There is no actual destination. Keep learning and continue to inspire others.

Make a note of insights, key learning points, personal recommendations, areas for review, books to read, actions to take, people to talk to and topics of interest you would like to research. Ask yourself the following questions: How successful was my last project? How did I recognize the team for their work? Who am I in conflict with and why? When should I schedule a recognition pit stop? Read a book written by John C. Maxwell or Dr. Harold Kerzner. Discuss and document success criteria with your project team. Peruse the very readable book by Judith W. Umlas, *The Power of Acknowledgment*, and determine how to put the "7 Principles of Acknowledgment"[4] to work with your team.

_____
_____
_____
_____
_____
_____
_____
_____
_____

Personal Leadership Activities
Table 1.1

Action Item	Target Date for Completion
Read another book about leadership	
Schedule a meeting with my project team to review expectations and develop updated project success criteria	
Plan to acknowledge my project team for the recent achievement of a milestone	
Seek a mentor	
Attend a class to improve my ability to influence people and create mutually beneficial relationships	
Conduct a 360 degree assessment to learn where I could make personal improvements	

2 Leading Project Managers and Teams to Higher Levels of Competency and Effectiveness

"It is followers not organizations that convey leadership. And before people will allow you to lead them, you must understand what they want from you and what they expect of you."
— James P. Lewis

Managing a project is a challenging job and it takes a person with a very wide range of skills to become an effective project manager. The project manager position also requires high levels of energy to sustain that effectiveness while managing and leading a project team. Most project managers will agree that the title "project manager" is actually a dual role — leader and manager. As Vijay Verma explains in his book Human Resource Skills for Project Managers, PMI®, project managers have several roles:

As a leader
- set direction and vision
- inspire teamwork
- align employees
- motivate and support

As a manager
- plan and budget
- organize work groups
- staff the project
- control the project[1]

For project managers to achieve greater levels of effectiveness and to advance within their organizations, they must continuously fine-tune their leadership skills. By doing this, they will also be fine tuning the skills and competencies of their project teams.

"Leadership" is defined by J.D. Batten, in *Tough Minded Leadership*, as "the development of a clear and complete system of expectations in order to identify, evoke and use the strengths of all resources in the organization, the most important of which is people."[2] In the project environment, the project manager relies on his or her team to perform the work, report status as well as problems and work together to achieve the project objectives. If we consider the people on the team as the most important resource we have on our projects, it makes sense to focus on their needs if the project manager wishes to increase the probability of achieving project success.

Project leadership can then be defined as the ability to get things done well through other people, to achieve the expectations of stakeholders and to deliver the project's product successfully through the team.

LEAD TO SUCCEED!

Here is a very simple way to look at leadership. This is truly Project Leadership in a nutshell – adapted from *Human Resource Skills for The Project Manager* by Vijay Verma:

L = **Listen** carefully and sincerely to your project team and stakeholders.

E = **Encourage** the heart of the team members (motivate them through action and empowerment)

A = **Act** (demonstrate your abilities through action, inspire the team, walk the talk)

D = **Deliver** (provide what you said you would provide and follow through on promises)[3]

Project leaders should continuously look for ways to improve their leadership capabilities. The Professional and Social Responsibility domain of project management as defined by the Project Management Institute® Role Delineation Study (recently updated in 2010) emphasizes the importance of lessons learned and knowledge sharing. These items apply to leadership also.[4] Leaders should look back at their decisions, analyze what has been accomplished, identify where improvements can be made and act on those lessons. A good practice is to ask yourself a question after a decision has been made and an action taken: Did that decision or action really accomplish what I had intended? If the answer is yes, then take a minute, think about the decision and make a note about why this was the right decision. Think about how the decision was communicated. Was it clearly explained? Did you listen to the feedback you received? If a decision results in a negative reaction, discontent, conflict and lower morale you may want to ask yourself: How could I have done that better? What factors did I miss? What behavior was I displaying when I made that decision? Did I have all of the facts needed to make that decision? It should be clearly understood that leaders do make mistakes. It is the behavior and the actions after a mistake has been made that provide a true indication of leadership ability.

Effectiveness and Competency

Improving the effectiveness and competency of the project team begins with the project manager. The project manager, as the team leader should have a very clear understanding of their capabilities and where they may need some improvement. It is therefore essential that every project manager develop a personal development plan. This begins with an honest and objective self-assessment. A technique familiar to many project managers and something that could be used for self-assessment is the Strengths, Weaknesses, Opportunities and Threats (SWOT) analysis. Using a SWOT analysis approach may provide the information necessary to design an ongoing self-development and personal improvement program. Assessing our personal strengths and weaknesses and identifying opportunities that await us, as well as threats that can inhibit us, will help establish priorities, especially if the project manager aspires to achieve higher levels of responsibility within an organization. Refer to figures 2.1 and 2.2 as examples of a Leadership SWOT Analysis.[5]

Leadership SWOT Analysis
Figure 2.1

Strengths	Opportunities
What skills do I possess that help me accomplish my goals? Consider what can be done to build even greater strength. **Examples:** • Communication • Presentation skills • Planning • Organizing • Listening • Facilitating • Problem Solving • Innovation and Entrepreneurship • Relationship building • Influencing skills	What opportunities exist at the project level, the organizational level and at the personal level? **Examples:** • Additional revenue and sales at project completion • New and more challenging project assignment • Sharing of knowledge with others in the organization • Promotion of team members • Promotion to higher level position • Increased customer satisfaction • Greater levels of personal satisfaction and self-worth • Coaching of team members

Leadership SWOT Analysis
Figure 2.2

Weaknesses	Threats
What weaknesses have I noticed or have been identified through feedback? **Examples:** • Failure to follow through on promises • Technical knowledge is limited • Slow response to team requests • Lack of visibility • Failure to provide feedback on a timely basis • Lack of availability to the team • Micromanaging the team • Failure to set clear expectations • Failure to fulfill promises and commitments	What threats exist that should be removed or mitigated? **Examples:** • Project failure due to poor leadership • Loss of job assignment • Loss of key project team members • Project cancellation • Loss of personal credibility and integrity • Personal issues • Aggressive peers • Difficult clients • Non-supportive sponsor or project executive

A leadership SWOT analysis will assist the project manager in identifying where additional training, support or mentorship is required. A similar approach can be taken with the project team. The key is to exploit strengths, resolve and strengthen weaknesses, capitalize on opportunities and remove or minimize threats. The action items developed to address these areas, when properly executed, will result in higher levels of personal performance, improved ability to lead and much greater efficiency at the team level. Leadership is something that is earned. It requires perseverance and genuine commitment. It is not about ego; it is about adding value. Continue to find ways to add value. Value is the key that opens the next door of opportunity.

Your Personal Leadership Action Register

Continue to develop a plan for your own personal growth as a leader. What insights within this chapter were most useful to you? What references are you interested in researching further? Conduct a Personal Leadership SWOT Analysis and use the results to help guide your personal development strategies.

Use the references in this chapter and any personal notes you have documented to assist you in designing a plan that will help you achieve your leadership goals. Make a note of insights, key learning points, personal recommendations, areas for review, books to read, self-development plans and topics of interest you would like to research.

_____
_____
_____
_____
_____
_____
_____
_____
_____
_____
_____
_____
_____
_____
_____
_____
_____
_____
_____

Personal Leadership Activities
Table 2.3

Action Item	Target Date for Completion
Create a personal development plan	
Conduct a leadership SWOT analysis	

3 The Art of Meeting Leadership

> "Meetings are indispensable when you don't want to do anything."
> — John Kenneth Galbraith

I have spoken with project managers from many organizations, industries and levels of management. When the subject of meeting effectiveness comes up, generally during discussions about communications, I ask a few simple questions: Do you frequently attend meetings that are basically a waste of time? Or, have you ever attended a meeting and couldn't understand why you were there? The truly amazing thing about these questions (actually it's almost frightening) is the surprisingly large number of people who answer yes! In every classroom or seminar I am facilitating, whether there are ten people or two hundred, the response is always the same. The majority of people appear to be attending meetings that are basically unproductive or unnecessary.

It seems that the business world in general is spending enormous amounts of money having people attend meetings that produce very little in terms of meaningful results. If someone were to actually calculate the amount of money spent on these unneeded or poorly run meetings, the amount might rival the national debt. What concerns me more is that people are aware that their meetings are unproductive, unnecessary or attended by the wrong people, and they still keep scheduling them! This is something that has to change if the project management profession is expected to be viewed as an asset to business.

I think it's important for project managers to develop and practice what I can only describe as effective Meeting Leadership Skills. I know of several project managers who run very successful and productive meetings and their reputations as project managers are extremely positive across their respective organizations. People who attend their meetings appreciate the coordination, the minimal non-productive time, the attention-to-time constraints and the preparedness of the project manager. These meeting leaders are demonstrating one of the many positive aspects of professional project management. Make no mistake about it, project management is far more than the ability to conduct a good meeting, but meeting management is certainly critical, and is an important skill to develop and keep sharp.

There are numerous sources of information about how to conduct a successful meeting. Most of them seem to include basically the same list of dos and don'ts. Based on my experience in the classroom and in the work environment, most people don't need to attend a two-day course in meeting management; they do know what it takes to conduct a good meeting, but sometimes a few helpful hints can make the difference between a meeting that adds value and one that contributes to the team's desire for some extra snooze time.

To conduct a truly effective meeting and to be perceived as a meeting leader instead of a meeting impeder, visualize your meeting as a project. That's what it is — a project with a start and end time, resources, constraints, purpose and a budget. Think as if it's your money and you want to get the most out of it by capitalizing on the time you have with your team or meeting attendees. Since you are the project manager of the meeting, you are positioned as the leader and the attendees are looking for you to set the meeting tone, keep them focused and control non-essential discussions and interruptions. Take charge and get your meeting off to a good start and start on time. If you said the meeting will start at 9:00 am, that's when it should start. Make sure you end it as planned also. People really appreciate when you manage time well.

The following are tips from people who have earned the title of "meeting leader" by reputation, as well as the respect of their co-workers and managers:

1. Food is a great way to get things started. Once the meeting starts, the food is removed. People who arrive late will not have an opportunity to partake in the refreshments. This will encourage them to arrive on time and it also sets the stage for a more focused meeting by removing the distraction (this of course will depend on the type and duration of the meeting, but food management keeps things under control).

2. Agendas are prepared and distributed well in advance of the meeting. Attendees should be able to review the topics beforehand and come to the meeting prepared.

3. The meeting purpose is specifically stated and only those who really should be there are invited (duly appointed representatives with decision making capability are invited when the key player cannot attend).

4. Start the meeting on time and set meeting expectations. It is generally not a good idea to read meeting rules to your attendees as if they were part of martial law, but some reminders about meeting etiquette are always appropriate early in the meeting.

5. Practice listening as much as possible. Do not interrupt people. This is a rule everyone should follow. Occasionally you will have to deal with a person who is disruptive, very vocal or in some way reducing the value of the meeting. Quick action on the part of the meeting leader is required to prevent loss of respect and damage to relationships that have been established. You want people to participate, gain from the experience and feel as if the time was well spent. You also want them to willingly come to your next scheduled meeting, so demonstrate your ability to control the meeting. There are many reference books and articles available about managing unruly or disruptive meeting participants. Invest some time and learn more about dealing with meeting characters.

I think the key is not to just act like you are in charge of the meeting but to be in charge. Be the leader, which basically means to be prepared. Make your team feel the energy and enthusiasm that you feel as well as a sense of tightness regarding how the meeting is managed. Immerse yourself in the role of leader. Time is limited, so make the most of it and respect the time constraints and other priorities of your meeting attendees. You want them to say as they are leaving: "Great meeting. Thank you, and when is the next one? I wish all of our meetings were this well run."

Meeting Leadership is just one of the many roles of the successful project manager. Set an example, set a standard. Your organization will appreciate it. Make it a point to have a reputation as a person who schedules and manages excellent meetings.

Your Personal Leadership Action Register

Continue to develop a plan for your own personal growth as a leader. Determine how you can raise the level of quality and effectiveness of your next meeting. What references and sources of information within this chapter were most relevant to your current assignment?

Use these references and any personal notes you have documented to assist you in designing a plan that will achieve your leadership goals. Make a note of insights, key learning points, personal recommendations, areas for review, books to read, self-development plans and topics of interest you would like to research.

Personal Leadership Activities
Figure 3.1

Action Item	Target Date for Completion
Obtain information about dealing with meeting "characters"	
Create a scorecard for your next meeting (analyze your meeting efficiency)	

4 Business Savvy and the Project Manager

> "It doesn't matter if your project is on time, within budget and within the planned scope if it's the wrong project."
> — Gary Heerkens, MPM, CPC, PMP, PEng

> "Fear breeds inaction, inaction leads to lack of experience, lack of experience fosters ignorance, and ignorance breeds fear."
> — John C. Maxwell.

By definition, the word savvy means "to understand" or "to be well informed and perceptive."[1] Another definition is "to have a practical understanding or shrewdness."[2] A banker or investment manager should be financially savvy. A CEO or a CFO should be, or have, business savvy if he or she expects to achieve organizational objectives and to be considered successful. In the business environment, success is generally based on how well money is managed and how much revenue or profit is attained. This means making the right decisions about where to invest capital, how to keep costs low and where the best returns can be expected.

Besides making decisions about schedule, resources, finances and costs, a project manager is also a business manager and leader. Basically, the role of the project manager is very similar to the role of the person accountable for business success. We generally classify people who are key players in the business decision processes or who have a significant position in an organization as leaders or part of the leadership team. That is a designation that may or may not be accurate but that's another story.

Leadership skills play an important part in the development of the business savvy project manager. He or she must be able to observe and comprehend a very broad business horizon and also contemplate what is beyond the horizon in terms of financial reward, risk and potential opportunity.

Businesses need people who can manage the company's financial assets effectively and determine where the most beneficial returns on investment may be found. In other words, businesses of any type need business savvy managers. In his book, *The Business Savvy Project Manager*, Gary Heerkens targets the project environment as an area where possessing business skills and knowledge is essential to project success.[3] If you ask project managers to define the criteria for project success, the usual response would be, in most cases: on time, within budget and within scope. But, as Heerkens asks, "Exactly how important are the objectives described within what project managers refer to as the Triple Constraint?"[4] The Triple Constraint, Figure 4.1, is generally depicted as a triangle with Cost, Schedule and Scope representing each side. Changes to any side of the triangle will most like affect the other two sides. The Triple Constraint is also used to define the competing demands of a project and the need to balance and manage these competing demands effectively.

TRIPLE CONSTRAINT TRIANGLE
FIGURE 4.1

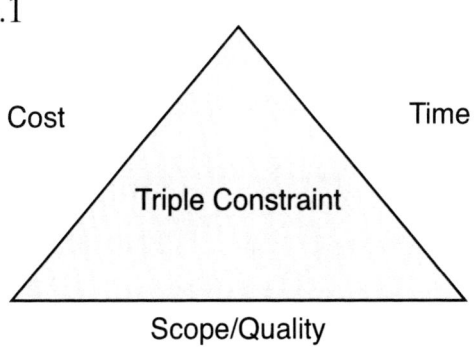

Cost   Time

Triple Constraint

Scope/Quality

Understanding the relationships between each side of the triangle is a key element in managing projects.

Certainly these items need attention and should be considered in the larger picture but there are other factors that must be included in the definition of success. An important item for project managers to consider (project sponsors and project executives should also take note) is that projects are financial investments and should be recognized as key elements when planning the strategies for achieving business excellence. This understanding of the financial implications associated with project selection, the possible benefits a project may provide (short- and long-term), and the connection between projects and the organization's bottom line will help to make a project manager indispensable to an organization. I think a goal of the career-minded project manager is to become indispensable to the business and to be considered a go-to person.

In the book *The World Class Project Manager* by Robert Wysocki and James P. Lewis, the authors developed a very comprehensive project manager profile designed to assist project managers as they further develop their project management skills and competencies. The profile provides the project manager with the ability to assess their abilities and areas for improvement regarding the following important skills:

- project management skills — sizing and scoping, scope statement development, the process for activity duration and cost estimating, critical path development and management, change control processes, monitoring and control tools and techniques
- personal skills — creativity, decision making, problem solving, team building and influencing skills, negotiating skills
- interpersonal skills — conflict management, balancing stakeholder needs
- business skills — budgeting, business assessment, business processes, communicating between multiple business entities
- management skills — delegation, managing change, managing multiple priorities, organizing, time management[5]

As you can see, the project manager must possess a wide variety of skills and demonstrate a high level of proficiency in most of them to be successful. Each of these skill areas is important but let us focus our attention specifically on business skills and organizational management. These include:

- budgeting — developing a time phased budget with consideration of direct costs, overhead, indirect costs, risk, contingencies and risk-mitigation strategies, the economic environment, international connections and miscellaneous costs
- business assessment — value of the project to the organization, alignment with organizational objectives
- business case justification — contributing to the business case and analyzing business case data
- business functions — understanding of business acumen and organizational processes such as procurement of goods and services, hiring, and change management
- business process design — how and why processes are developed and managed
- company products and services — what the company provides to its clients
- core application systems — the project manager should understand how internal systems interact and how they may support or affect the project environment and how the project may affect core applications
- customer service — providing, managing and improving customer service and achieving customer satisfaction
- implementation — execution of plans, managing resources
- planning: strategic and tactical — long-range and short-range; developing business scenarios and forecasting possible business futures
- product-vendor evaluation — selecting the most reliable and efficient suppliers and managing supplier relationships
- standards, procedures and policies — following standards, providing suggestions for improvement, supporting,

managing and enforcing core organizational policies
- systems and technology integration — system interfaces and interdependencies
- testing — verifying and validating system performance, quality assurance
- quality assurance — supporting the organizations quality policy and cooperating with internal audit procedures

If you compare this list to the Organization Process Assets and Enterprise Environmental Factors described in the Project Management Institute's PMBOK® Guide 4th edition,[6] you will notice a very close relationship. An awareness of environmental factors and the processes and policies that guide the operation of a business is essential for planning and executing approved projects.

Project Manager and General Manager – A Clear Connection

The nature of the project manager's job duties and the need for integration of project activities with business operations supports the belief among many that Project Managers are very similar to general managers (meaning they have some knowledge of many business processes). There is an expectation among project sponsors and executive managers that the project manager should possess the skills and wisdom required to make the appropriate decisions and achieve the desired project results while maintaining the integrity and brand of the organization. There is a further understanding and expectation that the project manager will remain flexible enough to accept changes that are beneficial instead of rigidly focusing only on the planned results. In many cases the planned results defined at the project start are not actually desired by the customer. Continuous communication with the customer along with good judgment and some business sense will help identify the real needs of the customer and the organization supplying the product or service.

The project plan is actually the project manager's guide (typically based on estimates and past experience) and is expected to change as more is learned about the project and the team fine-tunes the objectives. The business savvy project manager will continue to look for new opportunities, as the project progresses, that will enhance the financial position of the organization, increase the probability of project success and reduce the impact of negative risk situations. All of this is done while managing the needs of the customer.

Another major item, identified by Heerkens, is emphasized in this statement: "It really doesn't matter how well you execute a project if it's the wrong project."[7] The business savvy project manager knows that project selection and project execution are equally important. Organizations need a solid project selection process that considers the time value of money, generation of positive cash flows, connection to the overall business strategy, effective use of resources and the impact on day-to-day operations. Another important consideration regarding effective project management and being business savvy is that there are times when spending more money on a project could be a very smart business decision, even if there is a risk that you will exceed the original approved budget. For many project managers, the driving factor, something that has become a form of conditioning, is to stay within budget no matter what, without considering the opportunities that could be realized if some additional cost is incurred. Changes and additions to the project that may increase quality, improve performance or in some other way enhance the project deliverable would generally be worth looking into. It is important to consider that the solution the client is actually looking for is not fully defined in the scope of work. This could mean a necessary increase in the scope of work. Of course, a change in scope should be discussed with the client, the appropriate change procedures should be followed and the original agreement should be modified through the normal negotiations process.

As the project management profession continues to evolve, project managers are realizing that an ever expanding knowledge base and new skills will be required to stay ahead of the demands of the organization, the customers and the competition. A greater awareness of business issues and complexities combined with general technical knowledge will be a key factor in success. Knowing when to apply appropriate business principles and concepts will separate the extraordinary project manager from the ordinary.

Project managers will have to become more interdependent and less dependent on other business units such as finance and accounting when making decisions. We will probably see many more projectized environments, which will force the project manager to learn more about business for employment survival, if for no other reason.

It is absolutely essential for project managers to understand that success is no longer associated with "On time, within budget and according to scope."[8] Client satisfaction, profitability, impact on strategic objectives, reduction in costs, relationship to other projects and company operations, increased market share and opportunities for new products are all part of project success. It is also worth mentioning that project success may also be measured by a few additional, sometimes forgotten, items:

- The product or service is actually being used by the customer.
- The project team survived (still employed). The project didn't make the papers (in other words, sometimes no news is good news).
- The team is willing to work together on a new project.
- The team members are willing to work with the project manager again.
- Customers voluntarily offer testimonials and recommendations.
- Management actually recognizes that project management is good for business.

Today's measures of project success are significantly different than just a few years ago. The responsibilities of the project manager and the skills needed to achieve success have also changed considerably. As Ron Kemp, PMP, HP PMO said: "Our project managers work on projects with $50 million budgets."[9] That is the equivalent of running a large business. Business skills, therefore, become essential for the career minded project manager.

Are You Savvy?

Project managers need business skills and must become business savvy to survive in today's demanding international project environment. It's time to take your career to the next level and learn more about how your company operates and learn the language of business. It will assist you in managing single projects, programs and portfolios much more effectively and position you for consideration for advancement and greater opportunity. Savvy?

Your Personal Leadership Action Register

Continue to develop a plan for your own personal growth as a leader. Are you a business savvy project manager? What are your business management strengths? In what areas should you further develop your knowledge?

Each chapter in this book contains many references and sources of additional information. Use these references and any personal notes you have documented to assist you in designing a plan that will achieve your leadership goals.

Make a note of insights, key learning points, personal recommendations, areas for review, books to read, self-development plans and topics of interest you would like to research.

_____
_____
_____
_____
_____
_____
_____
_____
_____
_____
_____
_____
_____
_____
_____
_____
_____

Personal Leadership Activities
Figure 4.2

Action Item	Target Date for Completion
Clearly show how my project will affect the organization's financial bottom line	
Ask my project team how they would measure project success	
Develop a set of critical success factors for my project	
Connect with managers responsible for my organization's business operations	

5 Value, Success and Twelve Factors for Effective Project Leadership

"You know your clients are satisfied when they see your name on caller I.D and still pick up."
— Anonymous

Success is something that all project managers and teams strive for. The question is: How do you define success? I have heard quite a few definitions and some that would not likely be found in a dictionary. A quick check on the definition of success resulted in the following:

1. The favorable or prosperous termination of attempts or endeavors.
2. The attainment of wealth, position, honors or the like.
3. The successful performance or achievement — the project was an overwhelming success!

The definition of project success depends largely upon on whom you are asking. Another way to say it would be that project success is determined through the eyes of the beholder. Regardless of personal opinion and view point, the project manager and the client MUST work together, collaborate and agree on the definition of success at the onset of the project. In the book *Value Driven Project Management* (I'm proud to say I assisted with that book), project success is achieved when planned business values are met. These values include:

- internal value — organizational efficiencies, documented best practices, employee/management relationships
- financial value — ROI, cost savings
- future value — new business, expanding markets customer-related value - partnerships, business enhancements, greater profitability[1]

Many project managers and organization executives start the discussion about success with the Triple Constraint — the balancing of time, cost and performance specifications (or quality in some literature) and the need to complete projects on time, within budget and according to scope, but success is generally determined by how the intended end user or client sees the outcome and whether or not the project's product or service is actually used or fulfills its intended purpose.

My favorite definition of success is a quote I saw posted on a training room wall at a client location in New York City. It read: "You know your client is satisfied when he or she sees you on caller I.D. and still picks up!" Success relates to customer satisfaction and what the client perceives success to be. Client satisfaction is clearly important but project leaders must be able to assess success from several different perspectives. These other perspectives relate to the human experience associated with the project (teamwork, leadership, recognition, acknowledgment, respect, trust) and the value the project will provide to both the client and the supplier in the short and long-term. If the client is pleased with the results of the project and commends you for your ability to get things done but your team never wants to work with you again, would you consider it a successful project? If you delivered the project on time, on budget and within specifications but have to take several weeks off to recover from lack of sleep, stress-related ailments or other health-related issues, is that project success? If you miss several important family events and your family members haven't spoken to you in weeks, would you think that the project was truly successful? If the project is delivered according to specifications and the product is not used, is that success? If a project delivers a result and the benefits are not seen immediately, does that indicate failure?

Project success goes beyond the project deliverables and it's important to consider every stakeholder's view of success (including your own family). It is also important to remember that the true value of a project may not be seen for some time after the project has been completed.

Project managers do have to make some sacrifices occasionally. The uncertainties of planning and execution and the changes that can be expected will place significant demands on the project manager and team. The organization's executives will also have to share in some of the discomforts that may be experienced when delivering projects and managing project portfolios. It goes with the job. I think the majority of project managers will agree that most projects experience some type of problem and additional cost or time or requirements changes can be expected. It is important for all key project stakeholders to understand that there will be some setbacks and some need to change the plan. There will also be a few occasions where compromise will be required or where someone will have to give up something in the interest of the greater good of the project and the organizations involved. There should be some balance between all of the elements and factors that determine exactly how success is defined. When looking back at project performance, consider measuring the amount of discomfort associated with the project. Maybe there should be a discomfort Key Performance Indicator (KPI). It could help when considering the selection of new projects.

When discussing project success criteria or KPIs, especially in today's economic environment, the subject of value should be included. Of particular importance are the organization's Foundation Values and Strategic or Innovative Values. According to Dr. Harold Kerzner, Foundation Values include teamwork, communications, cooperation, collaboration and trust. These values, when recognized and encouraged, create an environment where organizational effectiveness is nurtured and can grow rapidly. Strategic or Innovative Values include maintaining a degree of market share, brand recognition and protection, satisfying government regulations, ethical conduct, maintaining corporate image, intellectual property and creating a leadership position within the industry. Building a reputation of sustained competency and innovative thinking are also key areas associated with Strategic Values. We can add to that list the need to include a mindset of sustainability. This means working not only to manage the organization more effectively which will improve the probability of continued presence in the market but to work smarter and with an eye on the ecology as well. The value associated with a sustainable future has become a key factor in how society views an organization.2

We all know that every project is unique and that there is no one sure method to achieve project success but there are some items that most project managers will accept as key steps to project success. While reading the book *The Field Guide to Project Management, 2nd Edition*, I was inspired by Chapter 2, "The Elements of Project Success" written by Jeffery K. Pinto. Mr. Pinto provides a Ten Factor Success Model for projects.[3] I adapted the model to focus on project leadership and added two additional factors. This model touches on what I think many project managers will agree are key areas for effective leadership and increasing the probability of achieving success.

TWELVE FACTORS OF PROJECT LEADERSHIP AND CREATING VALUE

Lists and templates (sometimes referred to as organizational process assets) provide an effective method for developing strategies and plans. Most project management offices and centers of excellence maintain a number of standard templates and resources to ensure consistency in project implementation. These templates and lists help to organize a thought process and can be very effective when working with a team to brainstorm ideas, or establish a direction in which to follow to solve a problem. A list of items that may be useful to the practicing project manager is provided in the following table. Twelve factors that influence or demonstrate leadership are listed in the left column. The right column is for your personal notes or actions. Make a note of items or activities that you may wish to investigate further or implement to ensure the factor has been addressed satisfactorily either within your project or within the entire enterprise.

FIGURE 5.1

LEADERSHIP FACTORS	YOUR PERSONAL ACTION
1. Project Vision and Mission – A clearly defined vision (the end result of the project) and a connection to organizational strategies. Does the team clearly understand why the project has been initiated? Are you committed and can the team see that commitment?	
2. Strategic Value – Understanding the market perception of products and services, technology changes, market shifts, changes in customer priorities, brand recognition, corporate image, regulatory issues, and intellectual property.	
3. Visible Support – Are executives and or project leaders accessible, available when needed, and seen often by the project team and work package performers? Does the project have obvious, clear and demonstrated management support?	
4. Emphasis on Planning – Having a plan is one thing, but plans change. Are you emphasizing the need for continuous planning and remaining prepared for new risk situations? Planning is ongoing throughout the project life cycle and frequent plan reviews are necessary to ensure that the approach meets the opportunities and threats.	

Leadership Factors	Your Personal Action
5. Consulting with the team and the client – Do you ask the team questions? This provides the team with an indication that you are interested. Do you ask for advice and encourage innovation? This helps the team or the organization develop creative thinking. Do you check with the client to make sure there are no major issues? This demonstrates to the client that you care and are committed to meeting their needs. Do you look for new opportunities and discuss ideas with the team and the client? This will enhance the outcome of the project and may generate new areas for revenue.	
6. Team Motivation – Keeping the team focused is essential for success. How do you motivate your team? How do you maintain interest and high levels of energy? What is included in your reward and recognition process? Do you inspire excellence?	

Leadership Factors	Your Personal Action
7. Assess Technical Ability – Projects require technical expertise. The team should have the ability and the tools necessary to deliver the project's product. How do you determine the capability of your team? Where are the areas that are weak or require additional support? What back up plans are in place to ensure technical expertise is available? How often do you assess your team or your organization's technical competency and compare with your competition?	
8. Client Acceptance and Exit Strategy – Defining client acceptance criteria and developing a strategy to exit the project upon completion (or at termination) is a critical item often missed by project managers and teams. What is your process for project acceptance? Do you have clearly defined project acceptance criteria?	

Leadership Factors	Your Personal Action
9. Monitoring and Control Process – Establishing agreed upon monitoring and control procedures at project start up will focus the team on objectives and reduce the probability of experiencing significant variances. Control from the leader perspective means to ensure that the team members are in control of their work. Leadership is not about controlling the workers or the team. Leaders should offer support, look for potential problems and symptoms, and assist project team members as needed to keep the performance of their specific assignments within acceptable limits. Planned and unplanned performance appraisals are useful in this area as well as formal and informal recognition and acknowledgment for work well done.	
10. Effective Communication – Keeping the team informed of major issues and change requests, recognizing the team for good work, encouraging team members to report "bad news" or problem areas, ensuring that objectives are clear and that the team fully understands the scope of work. The leader should practice achieving the "I get it" factor. The "I get it" factor is the result of clear and effective communication of information in such a way that the receiver fully comprehends the message" as in "oh, yes I get it!"	

Leadership Factors	Your Personal Action
11. Problem Identification – preparing for problems by initiating a risk management process, establishing a system for identifying problems that may occur or detecting problems that may have occurred. Encouraging team members to think it terms of "what if" instead of "what now?" Leaders encourage project team members to think in terms of scenarios. What could happen? Why? What action can be taken to prevent a problem? Encourage proactive or "positive thinking" about risk management. Prep your team to think in terms of prevention, contingency and mitigation.	
12. A Solid Project Management Methodology – Having a well thought out and accepted methodology provides an organization with consistency, greater predictability of outcomes, and more efficient use of resources. Take time to review your method and procedures. What is working well? Where are the gaps, redundancies, or inefficiencies? Work with your team and practice continuous improvement.	

These factors may not be new to many project managers but the model does provide a framework to build from and to develop strategies that can improve the chances of achieving project success. Most project managers will agree that the project manager is part-leader and part-manager. Additionally, project managers are also part-manager and part-doer, especially in the IT environment. The hard part is deciding which part should be done by the project manager rather than by others. As stated in several books written about the subject of leadership, managers do things right and leaders do the right things. It's the right thing to develop a leadership strategy for your project and it will help you and your team to manage project deliverables more effectively and ultimately to do things right.

The Difference between Managing and Leading

There are many opinions about the characteristics of a leader and the difference between leaders and managers. The fact of the matter is that most effective leaders are also good managers. The truly effective leader knows that a balance must exist between the roles and focus of the managerial side and the leadership side of an individual assigned to lead a project team. That balance, when managed properly, is the basic element that will result in team motivation, commitment and a desire to perform well.

Figure 5.2

The Leadership Focus	The Management Focus
Vision	Objectives
Selling, Influencing (what and why)	Telling how and when
Long range and strategic view	Short term and tactical
People (empowerment)	Organization and Structure
Democracy	Autocracy
Enabling	Restraining
Developing	Maintaining
Challenging	Conforming
Originating	Imitating
Directing	Controlling
Innovating	Administrating
Policy	Procedures
Flexibility	Consistency
Risk (opportunity)	Risk (avoidance)
Creativity	Conformity

Effective leadership requires a balance between what we know as traditional leadership qualities and the managerial qualities needed for an organization to meet strategic, portfolio and project objectives. It is important for the project leader to do an occasional internal leadership system check to identify areas where improvement may be needed or where current knowledge and or skills may not be sufficient to meet an upcoming challenge. Leaders should remain in a state of learning and should always be asking the question — how can we do this better next time? Leadership means making things happen. Ensuring that important, useful things are accomplished that will add value to an organization. Continue to check your value contribution. Challenge yourself to go to the next level. Create an environment where leadership is contagious and encourage others to help lead the way to continued success.

The Future of Project Management and Project Leadership

One additional point that should be addressed is the changing view of project management. According to Dr. Kerzner, project managers must adapt to a new and continually evolving environment. This means that project managers will be required to adjust their skills and enhance their competencies to meet the challenges that are forming on the horizon. These competencies and skills include:

- effective leadership involving a multitude of stakeholders with different needs and expectations
- leadership of virtual or distributed teams
- leadership under the auspices of governance groups rather than a single project sponsor
- leadership where the end result is a moving target rather than a stationary target
- because of the moving target, leadership in an environment where there are numerous and necessary scope changes i.e. leadership of change
- leadership in an environment where religion, politics and culture can have a significant impact on project success
- leadership where methodologies are replaced by frameworks which are custom-designed to the client's demands

These are just some of the changes that can be expected and they will affect project leadership in the very near the future. Considering the rate at which technology changes, the increasing levels of competition in the world market and the uncertainty of the economy, the best advice at this time is to prepare now.

The best bet is to discuss value and success with your project team members, obtain the executive viewpoint and blend these perspectives together. The view is different between the top and the people managing projects and day-to-day operations. Make sure you consider all view- points when it comes to defining success and create an integrated definition that everyone can buy into.

Your Personal Leadership Action Register

Continue to develop a plan for your own personal growth as a leader. Which of the twelve leadership factors should you focus on first? Is there a 13th or 14th factor you can add? How are you preparing yourself and your team for the challenges of the future?

Each chapter contains many references and sources of information. Use these references and any personal notes you have documented to assist you in designing a plan that will achieve your leadership goals. Make a note of insights, key learning points, personal recommendations, areas for review, books to read, self-development plans and topics of interest you would like to research.

_____
_____
_____
_____
_____
_____
_____
_____
_____
_____
_____
_____
_____
_____
_____
_____
_____
_____

Personal Leadership Activities
Figure 5.3

Action Item	Target Date for Completion
Complete a personal assessment of the 12 leadership factors	
Discuss the meaning of effective leadership with my team	

6 Redefining Project Leadership

"Any dream worth living is worth sharing with others."

— John C. Maxwell

Many people believe that the definition of a leader is someone who stops at nothing, uses people to achieve their goals, climbs to the top making tough decisions and living with the results while carrying the burden of accountability. Others define leaders as people who can inspire their teams and co-workers to achieve more than they thought was possible through motivation and trust without issuing any orders at all. We all define leadership in our own way but I think it's important for any leader to fully understand the impact they have on their followers and peers.

To help me to be more creative in my career as a professional trainer, I spend some time watching movies and trying to find those movies that contain scenes that can help illustrate the principles of project management. The movie, *The Last Castle*,[1] starring Robert Redford, clearly shows how a person, without giving a single order can influence and inspire people to achieve great deeds. Lieutenant General Eugene Irwin, played by Redford, simply used a technique of building self-confidence and self-respect among the men he was serving with. He quickly created an organized and determined team without ever giving an order. Certainly there are many leaders who do that in real life but we don't actually have the opportunity to see many great leaders interacting with their team members on a day-to-day basis and at a personal level. The movie provides kind of an upfront and personal view of the leader and an opportunity to see and hear how a leader inspires the people around while generating self-respect, confidence and a feeling of pride. No matter how you define it, leadership makes things happen. The leader causes people to act and leadership produces results. There is, however, a positive and negative side of leadership and we should be aware of the effects of both sides.

The negative side—these leaders manage to accomplish their goals by forcing their employees or team members to follow strict guidelines, company policies and organizational protocol. They inhibit creativity by minimizing shared decisions and participatory discussions. They speak to their subordinates in near dictatorial terms. Consider the leader as the individual who gathers his team together supposedly for the purpose of obtaining input before making a decision and opens the discussion with the following statement:

> "Team, now that you have heard my idea I just want to say that I'm absolutely, positively convinced that this is the way to go! What do you think?"

It is clear that the decision has already been made and this type of meeting is merely a formality and a façade of open communication. Statements like that usually don't encourage much of a response.

Leaders who fall in the category of negative leadership generally have very little trust in their teams, want to make sure that they receive all of the credit for results and micro-manage to an extreme degree. It is important to note that there will be times, regardless of leadership style, when there will be a need to make decisions without discussion or to overrule a team decision. These situations are governed by the nature of the issue at hand and usually don't allow for much time for decision making. It's certainly not a good idea to gather everyone together for a brainstorming session on lifeboat deployment when the ship is sinking. The leaders in the negative leadership category do get things done and in times of crisis, they may even excel at achieving the desired goals. They make quick decisions and can live with their actions. Sometimes these actions create very unpleasant situations for their teams or subordinates. The negative leader frequently uses hard-nosed tactics and threats to accomplish goals, instilling fear within his or her organization.

It is important to point out that a strong and controlling behavior is not always a bad thing. In a time of crisis we need leaders who are precise in stating what they want and can assess loads of information quickly. The World Trade Center disaster of September 11, 2001 is an example of this type of leadership. Mayor Rudolph Giuliani, known for his strong leadership skills and tight management style, acted quickly and decisively to bring New York City back together after a devastating event. He became a national hero but he was also transformed by the experience. He emerged as a role model and positive leader (Read *Leadership* by Rudolph W. Giuliani).[2]

The positive side—leaders in this category rely on a more participative style. Consensus-driven decisions and trust in team members are extremely important. Leaders on the positive side create partnerships with their team members, employees and associates. An atmosphere of free and open thinking and sharing of creative ideas drives decisions and interaction. Disagreement is expected and even encouraged. Conflict often brings out the truly important issues and paves the way for the most effective solutions and agreements.

There are, however, risks associated with this style and leadership approach. Sometimes the distinction between the manager/leader and the team members becomes fuzzy. It is possible for the team to lose sight of who is actually leading and the team can get stuck in perpetual "one-upmanship" or trying to "out lead" one another. It's okay to sit at the round table where everyone is equal but eventually the leader must resume the leadership assignment. Responsibility and accountability for decisions must be clearly understood. Roles must also be fully explained and agreed upon to prevent teams from infighting and stalling progress. Consensus leadership sometimes delays the decision making process and the leader must know when to intervene and how to intervene in such a way that the team is not discouraged or has members who feel that their empowerment has been reduced.

Leadership means different things to different people. There are qualities and characteristics that are common among leaders but each leader has his or her own unique qualities. Think about your own leadership style and assess your behavior from the team member point of view. In many cases, leaders are considered role models. If you are a role model, what behaviors would you like your team members and associates to pick up from you? In Chapter Six of the book *Leadership*, Rudolph Giuliani says, "Making the right decision is the most important part of leadership!"[3] How do you ensure that you are making the right decisions? What process do you follow when making decisions?

Decision making can be difficult but, as the saying goes, "somebody's got to do it." Part of the process, perhaps the most important part, is the willingness to make a decision. Leaders act and make decisions even when all of the information isn't available. I believe this is expected of people in leadership positions. There will be few times when everything we need to know is provided for us before we make a decision. It is also generally understood that leaders don't always make the right decisions. It's unfortunate but it happens. What is important is that the leader attempts to make the best decision and then accepts the responsibility that goes with it. That's where lessons learned and experience come from. Knowing if you made the right decision usually comes after the decision is made and the results come back to you for review.

To help you in your attempt to make the ***right*** decision, here's a quick tip that I find most effective. During a fairly sizable project I was assigned to, the core team was faced with a complicated situation and was about to make a very important decision. After much discussion we thought we had determined the ***right*** solution. During the decision process we actually failed to include a consultant who had the greatest experience in this area. Just before we were about to issue the directive to implement our decision, the consultant asked a question that, to me, has become a key part of any decision process. The question he asked was:

> "Are you fully aware of the implications of that decision?"

Clearly we had missed something during our team discussions and his question caused us to step back and take another look. That step back saved us from a costly mistake. When critical decisions are about to be made, it would be a good idea to ask yourself or the team the same question. It is also a good idea to involve a fresh set of eyes. This may drive some additional thought and produce some new and possibly much better alternatives.

In my opinion, there is a positive and negative side of leadership and it involves more than personal styles of leadership. Leaders may switch from side to side on occasion, depending on the situation and whether or not they are aware of their own behavior, but it is important to understand the consequences of our actions and our behaviors. Positive Leadership is certainly preferred but if you have to assume a position of authority (giving an order instead of a suggestion) and it could be perceived as practicing negative leadership, try to do it with respect and with some compassion for who you are about to give the order to.

One more item before we move on to the next chapter. Think about the following statement:

> "Because of what I have done today, my organization will achieve its objectives."

Think about what you accomplish each day. If you take the time to keep track of your accomplishments you may be surprised at how much you actually do each day.

Create some type of daily accomplishment journal and write these questions on every page:

What did I accomplish today? How did I help my organization? How did I make a difference or add value today?

Example:
Today I found a way to save $500 on the purchase of a project component. Today I assisted a team member in resolving a persistent problem.

_____
_____
_____
_____
_____
_____
_____
_____
_____

Because of what we have accomplished today, my team will succeed in delivering our project objectives. Make note of your team's accomplishments in the same journal. Ask yourself: What did my team accomplish today?

_____
_____
_____
_____
_____
_____
_____
_____
_____

Take time each day to reflect on what was accomplished and how your actions helped to bring about the successes of the day. Think about who assisted in each success.

Share these statements with your team members or employees and encourage them to think about how they have contributed to the organization and to the team's success. Encourage your team members to keep their own personal journals.

Your Personal Leadership Journal

Maintain a focus on the positive side of leadership. Avoid the dark side of threats, penalties and forcing. Continue to develop your personal leadership plan. Make note of insights, key learning points, personal recommendations, areas for review, books to read, self-development plans and topics of interest.

Personal Leadership Activities
Figure 6.1

Action Item	Target Date for Completion

7 Lead Like Everyone's Watching

> "Leading is creating value through ideas, through systems, or through people."
> — Kevin Cashman

It seems that just about every day of the week you can pick up a newspaper and read about another CEO, corporate officer, or politician that has been sentenced to time in prison for cooking the books or some other completely inappropriate or downright illegal action. Their actions caused tremendous losses for a company, disappointment for shareholders and a trip to the unemployment line for hundreds, even thousands of employees. These so-called leaders completely missed the boat on what leadership is. Instead of working WITH the organization and its employees, they focused their energy on their own interests and their wallets, pocket books and personal portfolios. They were not leading a company or their constituents to greater levels of success but they were successful in the areas of deceit and dishonesty. Try finding any book, publication or periodical that includes those words in the definition or description of leadership.

Most people, at some time in their lives, have heard the phrase: Dance like no one is watching. It means that we shouldn't be concerned about how people are judging our behavior or how we act. We should do what feels right and what makes us comfortable. Too many people stay off the dance floor because they fear what others may think. We sacrifice fun and feeling free because of the fear of looking silly. Expressing one's self without fearing what someone else may think is, in my opinion, an essential leadership quality. Leaders need to share ideas, think differently, and cause other people to look their way while not being concerned about judgmental issues and whether or not they are dancing in step.

While we need to spend less time worrying about how people react to our free-spirited behavior and occasional step outside the familiar, when it comes to leadership, making decisions, planning strategies and working with people to build or improve our businesses, it is important for the leader to lead like everyone is watching. Leaders are in the spotlight, in one way or another, all of the time and all leaders must accept the fact that someone is watching. Even low-key leaders or those who do not prefer the spotlight and try to avoid attention are observed and followed. An example would be General Omar Bradley. He was known as the soldier's general during World War II. He was a great leader at a difficult time. He made tough decisions, and he was very much respected by the men and women in the ranks. He empathized with the soldiers and always kept the mission in mind.[1] General Patton and General MacArthur were also great leaders but their style and desires were focused on being in the spotlight. They needed to be noticed and they relished it. It was a mix of leadership with a heavy dose of politics and personal ego.[2]

Today's leaders, specifically project leaders, must be aware that people are watching their every move, analyzing their actions and sometimes questioning their decisions. They must be less concerned about their egos and more concerned about their team members, the organization and the goals and objectives of the project. Today's project leaders must consider how their actions and decisions will impact the team or the organization. Project Leaders must be willing to make the tough calls and then stand behind their decisions. Inevitably someone will challenge a decision. But more importantly, the tough calls should be based on the needs of the business, the stakeholders and the organization, not on the impact to one's own personal stock portfolio or financial assessment.

Many of today's leaders by their actions have caused the general business population to redefine what leadership really is and to set new expectations regarding those we call leaders. A good place for the leaders of today and the future is to start with trust. If you have the desire to be viewed as a leader, start by building trust among your potential followers. Create a vision that the entire organization or your followers can get behind.

  There is a saying about health and diet that if you take care of the inside, the inside will take care of the outside. To the leaders of today and tomorrow, take care of your teams, take care of the people who do the work, take care of your followers and they will achieve the goals of the organization. Communicate regularly with passion and conviction. Don't distance yourself from the very people you need. To be successful, your followers must believe in you and what you believe. Demonstrate that you have values and consistently connect with those values. Show respect, show firmness and always be fair. Demonstrate integrity: It is by far your greatest strength. Listen with sincerity to your team or your followers, and continue to build trust, not through words but through your actions. As I stated previously, take care of the inside (your team or your followers) and your outside, that which is seen by most, (your leadership and ability to work with others) will shine brightly and inspire not only your team members but the many who are watching as you lead.

Your Personal Leadership Action Register

We all have an ego. Keep it under control. An ego that controls you can lead to some serious implications. Remember, as a leader you are always being observed by someone. Don't be afraid to try a new dance (it's okay to take risks). Just keep your team and your organization in mind. They may not want follow your every move but they may enjoy seeing you taking some new steps.

Develop a plan for your own personal growth as a leader. Each chapter contains many references and sources of information. Use these references and any personal notes you have documented to assist you in designing a plan that will achieve your leadership goals.

Make a note of insights, key learning points, personal recommendations, areas for review, books to read, self-development plans and topics of interest you would like to research.

_____
_____
_____
_____
_____
_____
_____
_____
_____
_____
_____
_____
_____
_____
_____

Personal Leadership Activities
Figure 7.1

Action Item	Target Date for Completion

8 Establishing the Roles of the Project Team

> "Individual commitment to a group effort — that is what makes a team work, a company work, a society work, a civilization work."
> — Vince Lombardi

Effective project team leadership is probably the most important factor that will determine whether or not a project will be successful. Without leadership, project teams splinter into smaller groups and slowly drift apart to work on their own set of objectives, resulting in a lack of effective communication, conflicting roles and responsibilities, redundant work and all too often, rework. If a project manager does not establish a leadership role and a clear set of responsibilities for the project team at the start of the project, it will be difficult to develop a cohesive and high-performing team.

A critical factor in conditioning a team for success is for the project manager to take the time to establish expectations about team performance before the actual scope of work and project details are introduced. The project manager is, in many ways, similar to the coach of a sports team. The coach seeks out talent, identifies potential in each player and plans to develop those players who need some additional support. The additional support provided by the coach is most effective when the other members of the team become engaged. The more experienced or skilled players create an environment of support that in turn creates a team-wide feeling of confidence. It all begins with effective leadership.

Upon approval of a project and the signing of the project charter, the project manager begins the planning process and with the team, maps out the project plan. In an ideal world, the project manager is given the opportunity to select the project team and picks the most skilled and qualified resources to perform the project's activities. More realistically, the project manager is provided with a pre-selected team or must settle for whoever is available at the time. A true leader will not dwell on who has been assigned to the project but will identify the potential of each team member. Imagine a project manager speaking to his or her team for the first time and saying "Well, you're not what I really wanted but I guess you'll have to do." How would each person react to a statement like that? Can you expect commitment and dedication to achieving project objectives? It is most likely that you will receive minimum support and will have to spend great amounts of time micro-managing or looking for replacements as team members seek other positions or projects that they feel are more desirable.

To create an environment that will encourage the project team to step up to the challenges of the project, the project manager should invest some time and effort during the very early stages of the project planning process to establish a foundation for teamwork that will create a greater probability of achieving team and project success.

In *Project Management – A Systems Approach to Planning, Scheduling, and Controlling,* 10th edition, Dr. Harold Kerzner identifies several team member roles that a project manager may encounter.[1] Team members may demonstrate characteristics defined as destructive roles or supportive roles and every project manager should be aware of their existence and potential impact on the project. The project manager's goal is to emphasize the need for, and encourage team members to fulfill, the supportive roles while discouraging destructive roles. The project kick-off meeting is an ideal setting to introduce a project manager's expectations around the supportive roles and also create awareness among the project team members about the undesired destructive roles.

Destructive Team Members
Figure 8.1

The Aggressor	Openly and continuously criticizes team members, challenges ideas, deflates egos and tries to eliminate innovation
The Dominator	Manipulates, the team, seeks out weaknesses and tries to take over
The Devil's Advocate	Finds fault in everything and challenges any idea
The Topic Jumper	Switches from one idea to another, creates imbalance and inability to focus
The Recognition Seeker	Always argues for his or her position, attempts to take credit for successes, thinks he or she has the best ideas
The Withdrawer	Does not participate, withholds information, does not get involved in team discussions and activities
The Blocker	Provides multiple reasons why ideas won't work

It is clear by the descriptions of these destructive roles that they would be undesirable on any project team. By taking the time to introduce and explain these roles during the project kick-off meeting and creating an awareness about their negative impact on the project, the project manager can set expectations about what behaviors should not be displayed during the project life cycle.

Explaining what is not desired is only a part of the expectation-setting process. The project manager should, upon reviewing the undesired destructive roles, immediately focus on the supportive roles.

SUPPORTIVE PROJECT TEAM MEMBER ROLES
FIGURE 8.2

The Initiator	Looks for new ideas, uses phrases like – "Let's try this!" or "I'm sure we can come up with a solution if we work together"
The Information Seeker	Tries to become more informed, looks for resources and supportive data. Offers to research information for the benefit of the team
Information Givers	Shares what they know, increases the knowledge of the team
The Encouragers	Shows visible support for other people's ideas. Uses phrases like "That's a great idea or "I can support what you are suggesting"
The Clarifier	Helps make sure that everyone understands an issue or a decision
The Harmonizer	Creates a unified feeling among the team
The Gate Keeper	Ensures that all information is relevant and the team stays focused on the issue at hand

Working with a team that is actively displaying and practicing the supportive roles described in the table will significantly increase the chances for project success. By explaining these roles at project start up, the project manager effectively sets expectations for overall performance and proactively encourages the team to establish an environment that will make the work of the project more enjoyable and possibly fun.

The key here is for the project manager, as the leader, to prevent the destructive roles from developing by actively displaying the supportive roles and acknowledging team members when they display the desired characteristics of the supportive roles.

Your Personal Leadership Action Register

Develop a plan for your own personal growth as a leader. Each chapter contains many references and sources of information. In this chapter different types of team roles and personalities were identified. Have you worked with a team in which some of these personalities exist? What actions can you take to address the potential conflicts? How can you prepare to manage these personalities more effectively? Use these references and any personal notes you have documented to assist you in designing a plan that will achieve your leadership goals.

Make a note of insights, key learning points, personal recommendations, areas for review, books to read, self-development plans and topics of interest you would like to research.

Personal Leadership Activities

Action Item	Target Date for Completion
Develop a strategy for dealing with the disruptive personalities on my team	
Research and obtain information about how to manage difficult behaviors	

9 Leadership Lessons Learned

> "You will have achieved excellence as a leader when people will follow you everywhere if only out of curiosity."
>
> — Colin Powell

Anyone interested in the topic of leadership can find an enormous selection of material about the subject in any bookstore. If you do a search online using Google® you will discover more than 37,800,000 items related to the subject of leadership. Documentation, ideas and opinions about leadership can be found in any type of media from CDs, to magazine articles, history books and seminars featuring leadership experts from every industry. The secret to effective leadership is offered by author upon author. The fact is there are more secrets to effective leadership than there are effective leaders. Why do we continue to see this unending stream of information about leadership? Maybe it's because we are still trying to get it right.

At least one possible reason for the unending source of material about leadership and the secrets of the effective leader is the rapidly changing work environment. The work force today is much more diverse than ever. That fact alone creates a challenge for today's leaders. The needs of customers, both internal and external to an organization, as well as the needs of the employees continue to change and evolve adding more challenges to the leadership role.

The changing world business environment requires new and advanced interpersonal skills to manage multinational work teams and employees. The demands of today's projects result in longer work days and more complex technology integrations along with greater knowledge of cultural differences. Downtime for systems must be minimized and schedule demands require project managers to become, as a matter of survival, professional jugglers. Global projects require managers to learn about different customs and politics and find ways to overcome cultural barriers. Technology is changing at such a rapid pace that before you can finish this book, your laptop, smart phone or iPad will probably be obsolete. The pace of change continues to accelerate with no break in sight. Customers are much more demanding when it comes to products and services and every organization is on a quest to find new ways to reduce cost while increasing productivity and improving the bottom line results. Organizations are focusing more on program management and portfolio management to effectively manage resources while trying to remain "lean" in their thinking and lean in the physical state of the organization.

The continuous changes in the business environment place heavy demands on today's leaders. Author Thomas L. Friedman tells us "the world is flat" an observation about how technology is creating a much more even playing field in the international arena and with the resulting gradual shift of work, especially in the service industry, from west to east.[1] This technology-based change is causing project managers and organizational leaders to rethink strategies and develop new skills for managing in a very different and complex playing field.

During my research about leadership and my attempts to find new material that would appeal to project managers, I listened to an audio book about creating teamwork. The speaker mentioned something closely related to project management that is also related to leadership. The speaker, Lee Shelton, said there were three phases to a plan: planning, implementation and evaluation, or "PIE." He said that only two of these phases were actually practiced by most leaders — planning and implementation. The evaluation part was rarely done and if it was, it just received very brief attention. His conclusion — companies are continuously "reinventing the wheel."[2] This observation is generally corroborated by many project managers I have spoken with over the past few years. When the topic about lessons learned came up during discussions, most project managers stated that although lessons learned were important, they did not have time to document and share their lessons learned because they had to get started on the next project or projects that were waiting for them.

Most people will agree that taking the time to evaluate a project after implementation is a good idea. The questions, what went well? and what can be improved? provide a foundation for obtaining a wealth of information for the next project team. Sharing information about what actions improved performance, explaining what not to do and what symptoms to look for can make a difference at the project, program and enterprise level, and it could result in enormous savings in terms of cost and time.

It is understood by most project managers and project leaders that each project is unique, and that what happened in the past may not have any bearing on the future, but in most cases the experience of a past project will help a project manager or team develop more effective ways to handle new challenges.

Taking time to discuss lessons learned is actually a valuable use of time. It only takes a few minutes to review and document a good idea that worked or identify problems and issues that have been encountered so that others may be aware of what to watch out for. Most effective leaders have achieved their status through lessons learned (or their experiences) and applying what they have learned. They made some mistakes, learned from them, evaluated their actions and developed new strategies. It's the continuing cycle of leadership. The books written about leadership are written by leaders who have lived through the situations they described. Basically any book about leadership is actually a lessons learned document. Leadership best practices are generally described through actual experience. Rudy Giuliani, in his book *Leadership*, wrote about September 11, 2001 [3] that was certainly a unique experience, and it is still producing lessons learned.

A key item to remember about lessons learned and best practices is that they are not a universal fit and do not work in all project or work environments, but they do provide food for thought and act as fuel for innovation. In today's work environment, innovation is a major factor in the pursuit of success and a review of previous lessons learned can stimulate new ideas or enhance ideas that have worked in the past.

Considering the value of lessons learned, I thought it would be a good idea to create a list of Leadership Lessons Learned that practicing project managers to could review occasionally, and hopefully add to as more projects are managed and completed and experience grows. As with any list, it is not complete and more lessons can be added at any time with no limit. Consider this list to be a framework and a springboard that will encourage you to become more observant about the lessons you have learned as a leader. Document your own experiences and knowledge gained and develop a habit of sharing that knowledge with other leaders, especially the new leaders you are mentoring. There is no limit to the number of items on the list. We know that every project we work on will be different in some way, so there will always be a fresh supply of lessons learned. During a seminar, while I was presenting to a group of project managers I asked the audience the following question: Why do you enjoy being a project manager? One response from an energetic and enthusiastic participant that made a memorable impression was: Project management is very different. It's like coming to a new job every day! That response further supports the notion that there will always be new lessons to learn and therefore new opportunities to grow as a leader.

Leadership Lessons Learned

Most project managers will agree that lessons learned during project implementation should be documented and shared. Leaders also acknowledge the need to share lessons learned. Here is a collection developed from input by several experienced and effective leaders:

- Set priorities and revisit them regularly. Things change. What is true today may not be relevant in the future.
- Continue to learn. Education never stops.
- Surround yourself with great people. You will not have all of the answers. Create teams of people who will seek out the answers and/or solutions.

- Whenever possible, listen first, decide later. Obtain as much intelligence as possible. Consider other viewpoints.
- Keep your commitments.
- Establish a clear vision and communicate goals and objectives.
- Remain consistent. Don't change your values and your message based on your audience.
- Demonstrate loyalty to your team members and employees.
- Retain your agility and adaptability. Learn new skills and technologies.
- Coach, don't control, your team.
- Create an environment where people trust their leaders.
- Narrow the knowledge gap between worker and management. Encourage workers to assume greater responsibility by empowering them.
- Assess the skills of the people on your team. Know each team member's capabilities.
- Sometimes the best way to lead is to get up and do it.
- Sometimes you have to change the rules.
- First impressions can be deceiving.
- Hope is not a plan.
- Leaders are the ones in the loop (stay informed).
- Providing timely, useful information is critical to team success.
- Remain visible to your organization's people. Talk to them. People appreciate visits from their leaders. It establishes a connective environment.

Your Personal Leadership Action Register

Develop a plan for your own personal growth as a leader. Can you add to the list of leadership lessons learned? Each chapter contains many references and sources of information. Use these references and any personal notes you have documented to assist you in designing a plan that will achieve your leadership goals.

Make a note of insights, key learning points, personal recommendations, areas for review, books to read, self-development plans and topics of interest you would like to research.

Personal Leadership Activities
Figure 9.1

Action Item	Target Date for Completion
Create a personal journal of my most significant leadership lessons learned	

10 How 'ya doin'?

> "Everything in the world we want to do or get done, we must do with and through people."
> — Earl Nightingale

Effective Communication through Feedback and Follow-Up

In New York City a common form of greeting is to say, "How 'ya doin'?" There is actually no expectation from the person offering the greeting to hear how the other person is doing. The proper response is to simply say, "How YOU doin'?" and then just keep moving along. No follow up and no details required. Not even an actual answer to the question. Communication does occur in this exchange and it does seem to satisfy a basic need to acknowledge someone briefly but, in the project environment, the project manager must engage in a more complete exchange of information.

Following up on commitments is something we, as project managers, generally expect our project team members to do. Direction is given, roles are assigned, control measures are explained and the team is expected to fulfill its responsibilities. With all of the daily activities and the not so uncommon unexpected developments that a project manager is involved with, it's reasonable for the project manager to assume that once direction is given and the scope of work is explained, the project team members will go about their business and take care of their work packages, assigned tasks and project-related items without any further explanation. After all, the team members know what they are supposed to do. You explained it, didn't you? It's not the first time that they have been assigned to this type of work, right? This attitude or behavior on the part of the project manager is based on the belief that once the scope is explained and a clear explanation of the project has been provided, the team will understand what they have to do and go about getting it done.

Unfortunately, as many veteran project managers know, this belief is wishful thinking and very risky. My mentor in project management, Dan Ono, PMP was a true project management professional. He not only talked the talk but walked the walk of project management, had very high standards when it came to his direct reports and advised his project managers, associates and students that there are two phrases project managers should never use: "I hope" and "I assume." He suggested, or more specifically, demanded that his project managers remain fully and completely informed about their projects and that project managers should communicate very effectively with their project teams. That meant knowing what was going on at all times (staying in touch and informed) and constantly following up with and communicating with functional managers and team members. The intention was to ensure that the project manager had the most current status and that if any new issues developed they were addressed and resolved as quickly as possible. This certainly is a best practice from my perspective. It is also a practice that all project managers should adopt and implement.

My inspiration for this chapter, besides the lessons I learned from Dan Ono, comes from a one page article in *Fast Company* magazine. The article is entitled "Don't Just Check the Box" by Marshall Goldsmith. He talks about the gap between "I say" and "they do."[1] What is suggested in the article is that while we may believe we have clearly communicated directions and expectations, in many cases, that assumption or belief just isn't enough to ensure that the team will actually perform the work or the task that was explained.

Something else besides clear direction and initial upfront communication is required. That something else is follow-up and feedback. The check the box approach means that once you have explained what you want your team member or functional manager to do, or communicated a specific direction to a subordinate, your task and responsibility is fulfilled. It is now up to the person assigned to the task to follow through and get the job done. Most project managers will agree that the check the box approach doesn't really work in practice and many times leads to a large assortment of new and potentially complex problems. These problems may manifest themselves as poor quality, incomplete tasks, confusion and misinterpretation of information to name a few.

A more effective approach that will improve communication and increase the probability of project success is a three step process:

1. Explain what is required to be done in a language that the intended audience will understand (this means that you should make a sincere effort to become aware of the region of experience and knowledge of the audience). To do this effectively requires a bit of homework. Whenever possible, try to find out as much as you can about your audience, whether it's an individual or a group of people.

2. Have the individual or the team members you are working with explain to you what they are going to do (verify the transfer of information). Have them paraphrase your instructions (try to do this as tactfully as possible).

3. Observe the work and then provide feedback about performance and results.

Using that familiar New York City phrase we can simply call this process the "How 'ya doin'?" approach. It may sound silly but in the project environment, it's what we want to know. The project manager will evaluate the information provided to make an assessment to determine the overall condition of the project. This isn't really ground breaking information, but the fact of the matter is that project managers, including managers and sponsors, put too much faith in their own perceived upfront communications abilities. Many people assume that they are crystal clear when providing information or instructions. This assumption can result in some very unpleasant situations. Clear and concise information provided to the project team through excellent presentation skills and use of the familiar communications model (transmitter–receiver and feedback loops) is an important part of managing the project. But in order to feel comfortable that the team members *know* what they are supposed to do, a mechanism or process is needed to follow up for the purpose of ensuring that the right work is being done by the right people and that it is being done correctly. Remember, the enthusiasm and commitment you are able to generate during your project kick-off meeting could be diluted shortly after the meeting by the pressures the team members will encounter from other project managers and managers who have different priorities and are expecting deliverables associated with other projects. A plan for following up with team members will help keep them on track and minimize the influence of others.

Another important item to consider is that during actual execution of an activity, a new or better way of doing the work may be discovered by the performer. Asking the "How 'ya doin'?" question could uncover innovations and generate new lessons learned that can be shared with other project managers and teams. Keep in mind that your tone and perceived sincerity are very important when asking questions.

Now, if we consider the importance of follow-up and feedback or asking the occasional "How 'ya doin'?" questions and their connection to project activities, we can see the relationship to the leadership aspect of project management. A project manager does have many roles during the project life cycle but the most significant role, at least in my opinion, is that of the leader. Effective leaders remain in touch with their team members or direct reports by asking questions, showing interest and providing support.

Additionally, leaders provide feedback. Team members really should know how they are doing. It gives them a sense of direction, boosts morale and provides an opportunity for planning improvement. If the expectations of the leader are not being met it is the responsibility of the leader to determine why and then develop action plans to resolve the issues. This is where feedback ties into follow-up. The project manager should establish a method for checking the pulse of the project and determining project health. Depending on the current state of the project, it may be necessary to review and restate expectations, provide open and honest feedback and take the necessary actions to help the team or the person recover and realign themselves with the correct project work activities and expected levels of performance. We can further relate this follow-up and feedback approach to project control. The project manager's responsibility is not to control the functional managers but to help the functional managers control their own work. An effective communications process that includes follow-up and feedback will assist the team in controlling their work responsibilities.

Here are some questions you can ask yourself that will help you target areas for improvement in the overall project communications process:

1. How is your information distributed?
2. Who gets the information? (Are the right people receiving the information?)
3. How do you know they actually received it?
4. How well was the message explained?
5. How do you know if the receivers will remember that you sent the information?
6. How do you know the information was absorbed and understood?
7. How do you know that the receivers actually believe the information is important and will act on it?

A good blend of follow-up and feedback can reduce the risk of experiencing low levels of productivity and performance, widespread team apathy and surprises later in the project. Make it a habit to ask your team *How 'ya doin*? and make sure they understand that you actually want to know.

Your Personal Leadership Action Register

Effective communication is critical to project success. Leaders must continually develop and fine-tune their communications skills. Team members may change, stakeholders have different expectations and there is no one-size-fits-all communications plan. Develop a plan for your own personal growth as a leader. Each chapter contains many references and sources of information. Use these references and any personal notes you have documented to assist you in designing a plan that will achieve your leadership goals.

Make a note of insights, key learning points, personal recommendations, areas for review, books to read, self-development plans and topics of interest you would like to research.

Personal Leadership Activities
Figure 10.1

Action Item	Target Date for Completion
Analyze my effectiveness communicating information and following up with team members	

11 WHAT PROJECT MANAGERS ALREADY KNOW

"If everyone is moving forward together, then success takes care of itself."
— HENRY FORD

The title "project manager" is universally applied to anyone who is assigned to a unique or special undertaking. A project can be any activity, from moving an office from one building to another, to the construction of a multi-story office building. Projects are found in the military, in non-profit organizations and in government. A quick glance around any business and you can easily identify several projects in progress with people assigned as project managers to ensure successful completion. These different types of projects require different levels of project management experience and technical knowledge. In addition, most project managers are expected to be effective leaders and well versed in negotiation and conflict management. Considering all of the very different types of projects and the skills required to manage each type, there may be a need to define project managers not only by an industry classification but also by a level of qualification. Eventually, competency plus knowledge and experience will be the driving factors in the establishment of levels of qualification and the selection of project managers, but there are some items that are common to most project managers regardless of type of project.

Consider the following information that I collected over the past several years from about 1000 IT project managers. Project managers were asked to respond to the following three questions:

1. What are the top five key competencies of a project manager?
2. What are the top five major roadblocks to project start-up?
3. What are the top five major issues affecting project completion?

The responses were collected, analyzed and produced the following results:

- Top five key competencies of a PM:
    1. communications skills — verbal and written
    2. leadership skills
    3. organizing skills — planning, time management
    4. interpersonal skills
    5. negotiating skills — diplomacy and mediating
    6. team building skills
    7. technical skills

- Top five major roadblocks to project start-up
    1. resource constraints
    2. lack of information — incomplete SOW, unclear objectives,
    3. poor requirements definition
    4. roles and responsibilities not defined
    5. unrealistic schedules

- Top five major issues affecting project completion
    1. scope creep/scope change
    2. no defined completion criteria/acceptance criteria
    3. technology — limited functionality, product instability
    4. failure to manage customer expectations
    5. poor project plan — poorly defined deliverables[1]

Let's focus on the key competencies. You may have noticed that two more items were added to the first list of key competencies, so we actually have seven competencies instead of five. The reason for this is to show where, according to project managers, technical skills appear on the list of priorities. This does not mean that project managers should not have technical skills that are associated with their chosen industry, in this case Information Technology, but the soft skills, such as communications and leadership, seem to be more important to most of the project managers who responded to the survey. Technical skills are critical to success and we need subject matter experts and functional teams with those skills to perform the work.

Ideally, the project manager would coordinate the work of the technical experts and would not be involved in the actual hands on work. There may be some disagreement about the technical skills issue but most project managers I have spoken with believe that they do need some technical knowledge to speak the language and understand the product and deliverables, but their main focus is to coordinate, manage and integrate project activities. In other words, project managers should be technically credible, having a strong foundation of knowledge about the technology and an understanding about how all of the project deliverables work together to produce the final product or total system. Technical competency would be associated with the subject matter experts and the performers who do the actual work. Project managers should also have the ability to ask their technical experts appropriate and well directed questions when issues arise. This will certainly help establish and maintain a high level of respect and confidence between project manager and the functional managers.

Considering the general project management environment, I don't believe there would be much disagreement about the list of key competencies. Maybe the order in which they are presented could be argued but most managers would agree that we need project managers with these types of skills. The list itself could be the basis for creating a project manager's personal development plan. Regardless of skill level, additional learning and skill enhancement is always a good idea.

Referring to the information about road blocks to start-up and major issues that affect completion, it is fairly safe to say that the items identified are common to most project environments regardless of business or industry type. With few exceptions, project managers experience these issues repeatedly. So, if project managers know that these are the issues, why are the issues continuously being experienced?

One answer may be a lack of attention from executives and decision makers. Another reason may be the middle managers who seem to filter information that travels upward and downward through the organization. It could be simply be a lack of appropriate communication between project manager and executive levels.

The project manager position provides an opportunity for the person assigned to obtain a significant amount of knowledge about an organization. The exposure a project manager has to the functional groups assigned to the project creates the opportunities to learn about the business. Understanding the business processes that affect the management of projects and how an organization is operated creates an advantage for the project manager. If the issues identified in the survey were communicated in terms of impact on the business and the bottom line, the language that executives speak, there is no doubt that action would be taken to address and resolve many of the issues.

The project manager could translate resource issues into specific risk situations and project costs, including contractual penalties, projected overtime expenses, customer dissatisfaction, impact on brand and much more. Unrealistic schedules can place an organization in a very precarious situation where priorities begin to change faster than resources can be moved from on project to another. Emphasizing the appropriate amount of upfront planning and the use of lessons learned can reduce costs associated with substandard work and cutting corners to make a hastily set deadline.

Project managers, in a very short period time, learn a lot about the organization they are associated with. This knowledge, if properly utilized could help an organization prioritize its projects, manage resources more effectively and eliminate or minimize many of the risk situations that could impact projects and the operation side of a business. Project managers know what causes projects to fail and teams to break down. Organizations can capitalize on that knowledge. Conduct your own survey about the competencies, road blocks and project issues. I am sure you will gather similar results. The results will form the basis for action. Translate the results into lost revenue, opportunity cost and projected savings if the issues were addressed and resolved. Take advantage of what project managers already know!

Your Personal Leadership Action Register

Consider the competencies and roadblocks identified in this chapter. Compare the information with your own organization. Are there similarities? What roadblocks to project success exist? Discuss these issues with peers and other project managers.

Develop a plan for your own personal growth as a leader. Each chapter contains many references and sources of information. Use these references and any personal notes you have documented to assist you in designing a plan that will achieve your leadership goals.

Make a note of insights, key learning points, personal recommendations, areas for review, books to read, self-development plans and topics of interest you would like to research.

Personal Leadership Activities
Figure 11.1

Action Item	Target Date for Completion
Identify competencies I can improve	
Assess the roadblocks I face with my projects and develop a plan to address them	
Connect with other project managers and assess the impact of the issues we face from a cost perspective	

12 Leadership Lessons from the Future

> "Changes in life are not only possible and predictable, but to deny them is to be an accomplice to one's own unnecessary vegetation."
> — Gail Sheehy

Make it so! If you are a Star Trek® fan, these are the familiar words of a very unique leader and captain of the Starship Enterprise, Jean-Luc Picard. As a fan myself, I have always thought of the Star Trek® series as an imaginative and creative look at the future, filled some very interesting examples of leadership. "Make it so" is a phrase frequently used by Captain Picard after a suggestion is offered, by a crew member or officer, about how to get out of a serious situation or to improve operating efficiency. The phrase has also managed to become a book title: *Make It So – Leadership Lessons from Star Trek, The Next Generation* by Wess Roberts, Ph.D., and Bill Ross.[1]

The television series may not be on the top of the list of sources one would seek out to learn about leadership but I believe we can learn a lot from the good captain and his crew. The writers of the program clearly spent quite a bit of time developing the scenarios, the challenges and the responses the captain and crew would develop to resolve the immediate crisis. The series has always been looked upon as being ahead of its time in terms of technology, ideas, creativity and especially the management of people. As an example, the series has demonstrated the importance of diversity and the ability of people of many races to work effectively together with an almost complete absence of prejudice. The phrase "Where no MAN has gone before," which was part of the opening of each episode in the original series, was replaced by "Where no ONE has gone before" for the opening of the Next Generation series of episodes. The initial series featured a white male captain. In subsequent series, the captain was a black male (Deep Space Nine) and later, the captain of the Voyager was female. There are many examples within the series where diversity was highlighted and the captain relied heavily on the talent and knowledge of diverse teams working together to resolve nearly hopeless situations.[2]

I am not suggesting that all project managers go out and purchase red and black jump suits, enroll in Star Fleet Academy and carry phasers, but I do think we can learn a few new skills from the series that we can add to our current inventory of leadership skills. If you think about the projects you are assigned to, you will realize that "Project Away Teams" actually exist: These are teams that are not at our specific location like virtual teams. We work with different time zones, different languages and customs and different approaches to managing projects. Star Trek may be based on fictional space adventure, but project managers must deal with situations similar to those experienced by the Enterprise crew. Customs may be different, laws are different, appearances may vary greatly, remote locations must be reached and what we say may be interpreted very differently from what we intended.

The series Star Trek – The Next Generation® is filled with examples of extraordinary leadership. There are valuable lessons about respect, acceptance of an individual without regard to gender, race, culture or appearance. There are many examples where the leader (Captain Picard) seeks the wisdom and intelligence of his crew members before making decisions or relies on them to act on their own, empowering them to make decisions (and sometimes, mistakes). As stated in the book, Picard is not perfect. He has flaws, as do all leaders, but the qualities of extraordinary leadership this fictional character displays can be found within those project managers who are committed to success, understand the value of their teams and have a desire to make a difference in the organizations.

In an article I had written for the newsletter associated with *allPM*, a website for project managers around the globe, I suggested that we need to "Lead Like Everyone Is Watching."[3] What I meant was that leaders should be as transparent as possible and that the eyes of many are always on them. Looking for direction and looking for an example to follow. Leaders should be consistent and understand the implications of their actions and be prepared for any fallout or criticism. Wess Roberts says, "It is the leader's responsibility to proceed with his duties without regard to being under constant examination. An awareness of the constant examination is necessary but the strong leader will make the most appropriate decisions and accept the responsibility for the outcome."[4]

Moving forward and getting back to the future about leadership, most leaders will agree that lessons learned through experience are important and can be of great value to an organization. Sometimes lessons learned tell us what we should do and what we should avoid. Sometimes they even tell us not to look back but to set our sights on the next horizon. Sometimes we should move slowly and sometimes we need to move at warp speed. Here are a few lessons, compliments of Captain Picard with comments by an "arm chair" starship captain (me):

Leadership Lessons Learned — from the Future

Leadership Lesson #1- A Federation officer is rarely more effective than the capabilities of those around him (or her). A principal responsibility therefore is to develop the leadership abilities of his or her subordinates (in our case, the project team members). Provide an opportunity for your project teams to gain leadership skills through additional responsibility and your trust. Arrange or support professional development programs. Empower your team members and focus on developing new leaders.

Leadership Lesson #2 - It is common for newly appointed officers to imitate great leaders. It's important to know that when you stop imitating and start leading in your own personal way, you will emerge as a great leader with your own distinctive qualities. Identify and connect with a mentor. It is not necessary to copy the actions and behaviors of a mentor but to find, within yourself, the qualities that will make you a mentor of future leaders.

Leadership Lesson #3 - Newly commissioned officers are intelligent but usually not yet wise. Arrogance, lack of proper personal discipline, ego and too much self-confidence often result in disaster. Lack of good judgment can be a hard and painful lesson. New leaders should fully understand their limitations, seek out advice from others with experience and consider their options carefully. One of my favorite quotes is, "Good judgment comes from experience, and experience comes from bad judgment."[5] We don't start out being wise but over time, wisdom is accumulated.

Leadership Lesson #4- Ambition can be costly. Leaders should not focus solely on the pursuit of rewards and career advancement. Remember ENRON and others? A proper balance of personal and professional life is essential for success. Relationships are an important component of effective leadership. In health care there is a saying that if you take care of the inside, the inside will take care of the outside. In business, it is basically the same. Take care of your people and they will take care of you.

There are several more lessons we can learn from the future and perhaps I'll keep adding to them over time. It is important to understand that there are many types of leaders we can look up to. Some, as in the case of Captain Picard, are fictional but their experiences are based on actual experiences, knowledge and research of the writers. Others lived in the past and we can only read about their accomplishments or see them acted out in a movie or play. Many more are working among us. Some may even be working for you. We should continue to learn all we can about leadership from as many sources as possible and identify those qualities that will help us emerge as respected leaders within our teams and in the profession of project management.

All project managers are "captains" of their teams and many teams are virtual, working in areas remote to the project manager's office. Look upon these teams as "Away Teams." Keep in contact with them on a regular basis and don't ever make them feel that they are disconnected. In Star Trek, the team that becomes disconnected from the Enterprise usually experiences some very unfortunate and challenging situations. They are off in some uncharted territory that is loaded with risks and the unexpected. How can you support them from a distance? Think about how you will answer the following questions:

- How can you provide them with the tools and skills they need to succeed?
- How can you communicate more effectively to improve the probability of success?
- How can you ensure that you are visible enough to keep them focused on the objectives without doing their jobs for them?
- How can you make them feel more connected to you, to the organization and to its overall mission?

Start keeping a captain's log for your project and record your successes as well as your weaknesses and challenges. By doing this you will establish your own lessons learned files and become a source of learning for the next generation of project managers. As Captain Picard says, "ENGAGE!"

Your Personal Leadership Action Register

Consider your ability to manage a distributed or virtual team. How well do you keep your team informed? How do you motivate new members of your team? Can you make a list of your own leadership lessons learned? How well connected is your team?

Develop a plan for your own personal growth as a leader. Each chapter contains many references and sources of information. Use these references and any personal notes you have documented to assist you in designing a plan that will achieve your leadership goals.

Make a note of insights, key learning points, personal recommendations, areas for review, books to read, self-development plans and topics of interest you would like to research.

Personal Leadership Activities
Figure 12.1

Action Item	Target Date for Completion
Establish a plan to ensure that my virtual team remains well informed and connected	
Develop a list of three or four leadership skills I can further develop	
Identify a mentor	

13 OYAKUDACHI

> "The leader for today and the future will be focused on how to be: how to develop quality, character, mind-set, values, principles and courage."
> — FRANCES HESSELBEIN

I often look for ideas about leadership by reading and reviewing articles in magazines, newsletters and other publications. Sometimes the connection of a particular subject to the topic of leadership is not always readily apparent and requires a little creativity. In other cases, the connection seems to be completely clear and it's a no-brainer.

I often read while I am traveling and I noticed an article, titled "A New World Order" written by Kathleen Carr about the vision of the CEO Oyakudachi, of Tokyo-based Ricoh Co., a technology company, and this article had a very clear connection to leadership. Oyakudachi means "walking in the customer's shoes." Most organizational leaders will agree that the success of their organization is directly tied to customer satisfaction and meeting customer needs. Unhappy customers seek other suppliers (they follow something known as the "law of two feet," which translates to "if you don't like where you are or who you are doing business with, just stand up and walk someplace else"). If too many customers practice the law of two feet, the customer base will begin to erode and if there is no response plan or mitigation strategy in place, the result could be devastating to an organization.[1]

To truly understand the customer, it is important to see things from their perspective. Many organizations call this being customer driven. Taking steps to obtain customer input about a product, analyzing their needs and then providing products and services that are user-friendly, meet functionality requirements, are reliable and acceptably priced are key success criteria and should be emphasized throughout any organization.

In the project management environment, the word "customer" refers to two important groups — the actual customer or ultimate customer — the person or organization that will receive and use the product of the project, and the internal customer — the project team members and key stakeholders. Yes, each project team member and, in fact, just about all the project stakeholders, can be defined as customers.

In the project environment it is important to remember that the customer is the next person in the process. Many authors of project management books and articles explain that project management is basically a series of processes that bring about a result. Most well-known experts in the field of project management emphasize the need to focus on the process and not the end product. The end product is certainly important but the processes in place are the critical success factors that will ensure a high quality end product. The process, if followed correctly, will produce the desired result. This is what the customer really wants and often it is not clear at the start of the project. It is important to note that the desired result may actually be different than the original planned result. We do need a starting point but in many cases the actual final deliverable is elaborated over time. It is the desired result defined by the customer, sometimes through several phases of the project, that the project team and project manager should be attempting to deliver.

How do you get to the desired result? Follow a proven process that includes requirements definition, validation of requirements, acceptance of requirements and change control, while looking for opportunities for improvement both in the process and in the product.

Some flexibility is needed in most projects. There is a vision of what is to be accomplished but that vision and the plans to achieve it are based on what was learned from past projects and by guessing and attempting to see into the future. New and better ideas could emerge as the project progresses.

Getting back to the statement, "the customer is the next person in the process," it is important for the project team members to view themselves as both customer and supplier. Each activity assigned to a project team member will produce, in most cases, a deliverable (a tangible, verifiable work output). This makes the person responsible for the activity and the deliverable the supplier. That deliverable is then handed off to the next person in the process who will use the received deliverable (an input to the next process) to complete his or her assigned activity. This makes the person receiving the deliverable the customer. The customer completes his or her assigned activity and becomes a supplier handing off their deliverable to the next customer. This process is repeated many times throughout the project. The supplier provides a deliverable to a defined customer; the customer processes the deliverable, performs their assigned activity and then becomes a supplier to the next customer.

To gain the greatest benefits from this process the supplier and customer should invest some time upfront, before actual work begins, and establish clear expectations and acceptance criteria. Setting expectations and defining acceptance criteria before work begins can reduce rework, frustration and poor quality significantly. This is where Oyakudachi comes in. Learn to walk in the customer's shoes by first asking what the customer needs. Actually view the deliverable from the customer's perspective. When an understanding has been established and agreement has been reached, the supplier should be in a position to produce what the customer needs with minimal changes and rework. This practice, if introduced early in the project and supported by the project manager and project sponsor should improve quality, enhance communication and, most likely, accelerate the completion of the project. Figure 13.1 depicts this model.

The Customer-Supplier Model
Figure 13.1

For each customer supplier interaction:
- Set Expectations

Define Deliverables – Agrees on Acceptance
- Criteria

(Supplier) (Customer Supplier) (Customer Supplier) (Customer Supplier)

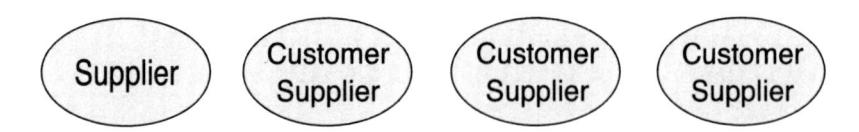

The hand-off of a deliverable from one functional group to another (example — design to build) is a customer-supplier relationship. Expectations should be clearly defined before work begins and acceptance criteria should be fully understood. The supplier should always have a thorough understanding about the customer's view of acceptance.

Most project managers will agree that customer satisfaction determines project success and success is achieved through much more than managing the Triple Constraint. It is also important to consider the satisfaction of the project team members who are all customers in some way. The Customer–Supplier Model[2], when applied to projects and supported by the key stakeholders, should result in higher and higher levels of team performance and greater levels of quality. An added benefit might be greater pride in the work performed and a feeling of true satisfaction among team members who have learned the importance of communicating expectations before actually beginning the work. The practice of setting expectations and clearly defining acceptance criteria may become a standard in your organization. Think of the possibilities.

Oyakudachi is a word worth remembering. It will give a project manager a greater sense of worldliness, while encouraging teamwork and better quality. It will make a difference in how projects are managed and provide leaders with a new perspective about just who their customers are.

Your Personal Leadership Action Register

Who are your customers? Consider anyone who will receive some type of deliverable from you to be your customer. The deliverable can be a report or presentation, or part of a system. Make sure you understand what is needed before you actually attempt to deliver.

Develop a plan for your own personal growth as a leader. Each chapter contains many references and sources of information. Use these references and any personal notes you have documented to assist you in designing a plan that will achieve your leadership goals.

Make a note of insights, key learning points, personal recommendations, areas for review, books to read, self-development plans and topics of interest you would like to research.

Personal Leadership Activities
Figure 13.2

Action Item	Target Date for Completion
Identify my key customers	
List all products or deliverables I produce and meet with my customers to find ways to improve their satisfaction	

14 Assessing Leadership

"It's hard to lead a cavalry charge if you think you look funny on a horse."
— Adlai Stevenson

Leadership, like many things, is defined from several perspectives and may have a fairly diverse and even controversial set of meanings. If someone is placed in charge of a group, an organization, even a country, that person is generally assigned the title "Leader." The headlines in the various newspapers that offer us a view of the world and its happenings often refer to heads of state, politicians, community activists and others who are frequent attention grabbers as a leader. A brutal regime focused on suppression of its population is often referred to as the leadership of that particular country. I question whether those who are in control by means of force or political connection are actually leaders. Leadership is defined by one's own personal values, culture and, in many cases, what the general population may accept.

So what is leadership? How do we define it? How do we assess the competency of leaders? How do we determine who the true leaders are? Try this brief experiment: Gather a small group of people, maybe your project team, and ask them to identify the characteristics of a leader. You can do this by simply brainstorming to develop a list of these characteristics. To help them with this exercise, ask each member of the group to think of someone they personally believe to be a true leader. What characteristics are displayed or actions taken that cause one to think this person is a leader? Chances are you will soon have a list of skills and characteristics that include communication, negotiation, presentation, interpersonal, charisma, confidence, decision-making, visionary, mentor, coach, emotional intelligence, intellect and perhaps several more.

There is no doubt that effective leaders possess many of these skills, but can you have all of these and still fall short of effective leadership? I think the answer is yes. I believe that true leadership starts with one's desire to add value to his or her organization, to make a difference, to contribute in such a way that other people are inspired to step up to new challenges and make their own contributions. If we look back at the headlines over the past few years, we can see that people who were given the title of leader fell far short in the area of contribution and adding value. These leaders were given their positions because they looked good or were well spoken, or had charisma and charm. Confidence in corporate leaders has been shaken because these so-called leaders didn't do what they promised. Their vision was focused on themselves.

Leadership means commitment to a team or an organization. It's about determining what's best for an organization by listening, gathering information, analyzing alternatives, respecting the opinions of others and asking for help. Leaders don't have all the answers. True leaders know that and look to their associates, co-workers, team members or employees for ideas and answers.

Assessing our Leadership Qualities

For most of us, a manager or someone to whom we report assesses our competencies. For some, it's the client, for others, it's the boss (coach in some companies) making the assessment. The question is, does this assessment include leadership capabilities? Take a close look at your appraisal or evaluation form. How is leadership being assessed? Most appraisal forms are focused on results, completion of objectives and customer satisfaction. Character may be included but it's generally a small part, mainly because it is a very subjective area. So how do we assess our leadership ability and potential?

Here's one approach. Take some time at the end of the day or the end of the week. Think about what you accomplished. What *did* you accomplish? Many people tell me they can't remember everything they did during the day, let alone the week! Okay. So start keeping a journal. At the end of the day, look back about eight hours and recall what you did. What meetings did you attend? Who did you speak with? What decisions did you make? Who was affected by that decision? How did you contribute to the organization? What conflicts did you encounter? Did you criticize someone? Why? What was the reason? What was the outcome? Did you inspire someone? How? Did you insult someone? Was it really necessary? Did you have an argument? How did you behave? Did you ever say to yourself after meeting with an individual, well, that could have gone better! What did you learn from that experience that will help you improve your approach and produce a more favorable outcome if there is a next time? Did you share an idea or encourage someone who had an idea? Did you enjoy the day? Why? Why not? What will you do to make tomorrow different? Answering these questions on a daily or weekly basis will help you to assess your leadership ability and cause you to think about how you can improve your skills.

Leadership is not assessed by charisma or good looks. It is assessed through actions that benefit the organization. Leaders make a difference. They are also aware of their surroundings and the impact their decisions will have on others. Leaders are required to make difficult decisions and often their actions are highly criticized. The true leader is ready to make those decisions and accept the results. When assessing leadership, think in terms of what has changed. What new opportunities have been created or what problems have been avoided? There may be some discomfort experienced as a result of a decision but consider the consequences if a decision was not made.

I remember a speech given at a Project Management Institute (PMI®) symposium where the speaker, near the end of his presentation about leadership, asked the question: "When you leave this earth, will you leave a vacancy or a void?"[1] Leaders leave voids. Voids are difficult to fill and people notice the void for a long period of time. Regardless of your position on a project, you can be a leader. Make a contribution and add value to your team. Continue to develop your leadership characteristics and skills. Think like a leader. Find a mentor who can help you on your leadership journey. Become a mentor for an aspiring leader.

Consider what you do each day and make it a point to focus on those actions that add value and create opportunity for your organization. Anytime you perform an action that benefits your team, your organization, your customers or your peers, you are leading. We need more leadership-based organizations. You don't have to do one great thing. Many leaders are known for their many small contributions that collectively made a significant difference. You accomplish quite a bit each day. Use those accomplishments to energize the leader within you to continue on a path of contribution. Your actions will ignite the desire in others to step up to their own leadership potential.

Your Personal Leadership Action Register

What leadership qualities to you display each day? Think about how you contribute during a meeting. Do you show enthusiasm when working with a team? Do you encourage others to work together to solve a problem. Do you offer new ideas and innovative ways to achieve objectives? These are all acts of leadership.

Develop a plan for your own personal growth as a leader. Each chapter contains many references and sources of information. Use these references and any personal notes you have documented to assist you in designing a plan that will achieve your leadership goals.

Make a note of insights, key learning points, personal recommendations, areas for review, books to read, self-development plans and topics of interest you would like to research.

_____
_____
_____
_____
_____
_____
_____
_____
_____
_____
_____
_____
_____
_____
_____
_____

Personal Leadership Activities
Figure 14.1

Action Item	Target Date for Completion
Identify my greatest leadership attributes	
Attend a training program about leadership	
Research great leaders and identify their common characteristics	

15 The Importance of Creativity in the Project Team

"You do not lead by hitting people over the head — that's assault, not leadership."
— Dwight D. Eisenhower

Most project managers will agree that the world is continually changing. New technology, new methods of travel, new products and even new languages based on internet chat and text messaging. New products and new ways of doing some things are the result of creative thought, sometimes from an individual and sometimes from a team of people. Creativity is actually a basic ingredient in the search for improved processes, solving problems and finding better ways to complete assignments. In fact, without some creative thought, life itself would be very bland. In the project environment, creativity plays an important part in completing the project. With tight schedules, limited funding and very often a lack of the resources that are needed, the project manager and project team must become entrepreneurs and innovators to complete the project objectives and meet stakeholder expectations. This requires creativity, a skill that should be included in the description of an effective leader and should be encouraged and developed within a project team.

When you think about people who are creative, who comes to mind? Artists, musicians, magicians, craftspeople, home decorators, clothing designers, architects, etc? These people are certainly creative: Their livelihood depends on it. What about project managers? Think about your past experiences. Have you ever had to find a solution to a problem or develop a work around in response to an unplanned event? Do you remember the solution and how you arrived at it? Although many people consider themselves as not being very creative, the fact is, we are all creative and just need something to set the process in motion.

In his book, *A Whack on the Side of the Head*, Roger von Oech, the author, provides some thoughts about how you can be more creative. He starts by asking the following questions: *When was the last time you had a creative idea? What was it?* Think about it. Can you remember being creative while working on a recent project? What motivates you to be creative? Did you face a significant challenge and had to come up with a solution fast? Think about those questions and answer them to yourself. Chances are you did have an opportunity to think creatively, if even for a brief moment.[1]

If you look at your environment and think that everything is fine as is, there is no reason to change. What has worked in the past is good enough. The organization can fall into a serious state of complacency. If all the rules in place are acceptable, nothing will be challenged and not much will happen. So why is creativity needed? For many reasons, two of which have been provided in von Oech's book, change for one. If change occurs, new information comes into existence. The second reason is we can't solve today's problems with yesterday's solutions. We need to look for fresh solutions to new problems. Lessons learned certainly have their value, but it is important to combine those lessons learned with new ideas so we can continue to move forward.[2]

Creativity can also add fun to the project environment. Generating ideas to solve problems, improve a process or creating a new product can be very enjoyable and help build the team, while improving the work environment. As with projects, ideas have life cycles. They are born, then developed, modified, executed and eventually live out their useful life. Therefore creative thinking is necessary to keep a fresh supply of ideas on hand. As von Oech says, knowledge is the stuff from which new ideas are born, so project leaders should continue to increase their knowledge about all facets of their business and then look beyond to other areas.[3] Sometimes knowledge about a subject unrelated to the project you are working on can actually stimulate new ways of thinking. Here's an example: I was reviewing a book about emergency medical training. I reviewed the triage and CPR (Cardio-Pulmonary Resuscitation) processes and techniques, and from those techniques developed a presentation entitled "CPR for IT Projects" or "Critical Path Resuscitation." I used the techniques of emergency treatment for patients to explain how to get a project in trouble on the road to recovery. First, focus on stabilizing and addressing the most important factors. Then conduct a detailed diagnosis and follow-up with a plan for recovery.

Von Oech said, "Discovery consists of looking at the same thing as everyone else and thinking something different."[4] He offers many ways to become more creative, but there is one thought he mentioned that we should always keep in mind, which is to look for the second right answer. There are always alternatives to a situation, so ask the what-if questions. Don't be afraid to sound a little silly. A great idea may be just waiting to jump out.

In his book, von Oech discusses what he calls "Mental Locks," things that prevent us from being creative. These Mental Locks are:

- the right answer (thinking that there is only one)
- always being logical
- follow the rules
- be practical
- play is frivolous
- that's not my area (or job)
- avoid ambiguity
- don't be foolish
- to err is wrong
- I'm not creative[5]

Each of these Mental Locks can prevent us from developing that much needed new technique, solving that persistent problem, improving how work is done or meeting a customer expectation.

As a project manager and leader, it is our job to observe the action, look for opportunities and work with our teams to resolve issues, so we can complete our assignments successfully. Creativity is part of the job, and we owe it to ourselves, our teams and our customers to continue to develop our creative edge. So take von Oech's advice: Give yourself a *Whack on the Side of the Head* and unlock that creative potential. You'll be surprised at the number of ideas that have been waiting for an opportunity to be born.

Your Personal Leadership Action Register

Everyone is creative to some degree. Sometimes are creative abilities are locked away or forced into submission by life's daily challenges. Try to use your imagination. Look at problems from a difference perspective. Daydream once in a while. Find ways to have fun while working with your project team.

Develop a plan for your own personal growth as a leader. Each chapter contains many references and sources of information. Use these references and any personal notes you have documented to assist you in designing a plan that will achieve your leadership goals. Make a note of insights, key learning points, personal recommendations, areas for review, books to read, self-development plans and topics of interest you would like to research.

Personal Leadership Activities
Figure 15.1

Action Item	Target Date for Completion
Read a book about creative problem solving	
Learn something new about your organization	
Learn about the hobbies of your team members	
Have a brainstorming session or group creativity session to generate new ideas to solve persistent problems	

16 The Future's So Bright, We Gotta Wear Shades

> "Leadership can be thought of as a capacity to define oneself to others in a way that clarifies and expands a vision of the future."
> — Edwin H. Friedman

You may recall the song title (and also the chapter title) if you think back a decade or two. The song suggested that we prepare ourselves for the great things we can expect to happen. It was upbeat and created a positive outlook. We need to think the same way about project management and the business environment. We have had some rough times in the recent past and for a while it didn't look like things would change much. There are lots of global issues, economic problems, unemployment, deceptive leadership and lack of trust. These issues are not new, and generally we cycle through them into new phases that are more encouraging and uplifting. As project managers, we should always be thinking about the current phase of our projects, but also have an eye looking towards the next phase. There isn't much time to dwell on the past. Take a glimpse through the project rear view mirror, jot down some lessons learned and then get your project in gear. We may not be able to predict the future, but we can take actions that will influence it.

Project managers have to make things happen. We are leaders and leaders don't sit around waiting for directions. Leaders set direction. Leaders set the vision, instill that vision in their teams and then work with them to achieve the goals. In other words, leaders lay out the plans for the future, and we need to paint a very bright picture of that future if we expect our teams to follow us. Focusing on the negatives and dark side of project management or the business world won't gain a lot of enthusiastic support. If you have been reading about new trends in project management, you may have noticed the increased emphasis on leadership, relationship building and the soft side of project management. Many project managers are attending programs, conferences and workshops aimed at improving their interpersonal skills and their ability to influence and motivate their team members. Motivation is the key to a successful project and a highly performing team. The soft skills help achieve significant results by creating pride, self-respect and self-worth about the work being done by the team. The ability of the leader to maintain a positive outlook and see opportunity even during the gloomiest of times is a difficult but essential skill.

Soft skills are certainly important, but soft skills alone will not guarantee project success or ensure effective leadership. The project manager of the future will require a very broad range of skills. The future project manager will become more effective and productive through the use of technology and by gaining a better understanding of business needs, direction and processes. Future project managers will think like and speak in the language of executive management and act like the CEO of the project while establishing a working relationship with project teams to deliver results that impact strategic goals. In the July 2003 issue of *PM Network* magazine, there is an article in the executive notebook section written by Joan Knutson entitled, "A Project Management Renaissance: The Future is Already Here." Knutson suggests that today's project managers are already reshaping the future with new ways to manage projects. The current economic conditions have impacted the profession of project management, and it is changing much faster as project managers fuel the movement to newer and smarter ways of managing projects. In her article, she discusses how projects are changing business cultures, how new techniques and options are being used to fast-track projects and how project management is becoming more strongly connected to strategic planning. Today, it is plain to see that Knutson's observations are right on target.[1]

It's true that we can't predict the future but, as project managers, we can take on a positive perspective. A favorite quote by Louis

Pasteur keeps me thinking about how we can influence an outcome: "Chance favors the prepared mind." [2] Louis Pasteur suggests that it isn't luck that caused something to turn out well; It's because we prepared ourselves for the possibilities and were ready to act on them when the time was right. As project managers, we need to keep looking toward the future with an occasional look in the rearview mirror. It should not be a long look back, as that could be dangerous. If we look behind us too long and too often, we will certainly miss a new opportunity or hit something we couldn't see because our focus was in the wrong direction. We do need to learn from our past and we do need to identify what can be done better, but make sure you manage that time wisely, and then get quickly back to the future, as the well-known movie title suggests. So, keep your eyes on the road ahead.

Preparing yourself to be the project manager of the future won't be difficult as long as you keep up with the latest trends, continue to educate yourself and improve your skills (especially interpersonal skills). Innovation and creativity will be key ingredients for success, so open up your mind to new techniques or challenge existing processes and methods. Look for a better way, not necessarily a new way, but look for an opportunity to change what is currently accepted. In most cases, we can find areas for improvement in just about everything we do.

Some suggestions that will help you prepare for the future:

1. Continued education and training. Not because your organization requires you to obtain 40 hours of training each year, but because you have a desire to learn. Pick subjects that will have an impact on what you do now. Learn new ways to do the things you do. Training and education are an investment in your future. Learning more about your organization and about business in general will increase your personal self-worth. The more you learn, the more interesting you become. Your network will expand and you will become a go-to person in your organization

or industry. People will seek your advice and new opportunities will develop almost magically.

2. Look back at what you have accomplished. Use your personal careerear view mirror on occasion to see where you were and what you have accomplished. Look at the more difficult times also and how you managed to resolve them. Caution, though — don't spend too much time in the past, as you can't change it. Just reflect on it and the lessons you learned from it. Use the past to help prepare yourself for the next set of adventures waiting for you on life's journey.

3. Become more aware of potential risks. There is no substitute for due diligence. Ask yourself a lot of what-if questions and think in terms of risk strategies. Always have a plan B. If you are leading a team, ask for suggestions, input and insight. Obtain multiple perspectives. Use the experience of your team and its synergy to become more prepared for the uncertainties of the future.

4. Don't wait for something to occur. Catch-up is not part of a leader's career path. Use your creativity and innovative skills to create opportunity.

5. Think like a CEO. Your project is a business in itself. Treat it like you are spending your own money.

6. Prepare for change. Don't resist it. Accept it. Cause it. Ensure that your team becomes change-ready. Focus on what you can influence in some way and concentrate your efforts there. Don't burn your energy in areas where you know you have no control at all.

7. Keep your eyes on the road ahead of you. Quick glances back are okay, but you really need to see what's ahead and what obstacles, hazards or opportunities are waiting for you. They sometimes appear without warning. You need to know when to change lanes, slow down, accelerate and even stop to refuel. Sometimes maintenance (your personal maintenance) will be required and that should be planned for. Make sure you know when to get a personal tune-up.

8. Surround yourself with a high-performing team and the experts that can get the job done. Build the team, reward the team and listen to the team. Without them you won't get very far.

9. Exercise adaptive leadership. The challenges of tomorrow will require fresh, bold and innovative thinking. Remain flexible and maintain an awareness of the business environment. Leaders are often required to switch gears with little notice.

The future is as bright as you want to make it. Don't let the future grab you and take you there: Make it happen. Direct it as much as you can. Create a vision for the near and the more distance future and create your future map. Put on those shades, fire up your imagination and your team and light up a path to success. Take advantage of today's technology to give you an edge, and be prepared to adapt to the new technologies that appear daily.

Your Personal Leadership Action Register

Develop a plan for your own personal growth as a leader. Create a vision of your personal future. Consider where you would like to be six months from now and two years from now. Be realistic but don't underestimate your capabilities.

Each chapter contains many references and sources of information. Use these references and any personal notes you have documented to assist you in designing a plan that will achieve your leadership goals. Make a note of insights, key learning points, personal recommendations, areas for review, books to read, self-development plans and topics of interest you would like to research.

_____
_____
_____
_____
_____
_____
_____
_____
_____
_____
_____
_____
_____
_____
_____
_____
_____
_____
_____
_____

Personal Leadership Activities
Figure 16.1

Action Item	Target Date for Completion
Create my personal vision and set specific goals that will guide me toward achieving that vision	

17 Retaining Your Key Team Members

> "What you always do before you make a decision is consult. The best public policy is made when you are listening to people who are going to be impacted. Then, once policy is determined, you call on them to help you sell it."
> — Elizabeth Dole

There are many characteristics of a leader, but there is undoubtedly one skill that every leader must possess to remain a leader: The ability to retain the key players of a team. It is one thing to build a team, which can be a formidable challenge depending on the situation and the environment, but it can be an even greater challenge to sustain a team and keep the team members focused on the objectives. The leader must establish a willingness among all team members to continue to work together towards greater goals and higher levels of accomplishment. If you think of high performance teams that you have been a member of or have observed in action, you will recall the strong sense of direction, purpose and the internal support structure of the team. There is a team-wide desire to succeed, but an even greater desire to work together. Great teams achieve their greatness by building trust, by demonstrating to each team member that everyone is important and by creating a sense of personal value and contribution for each member.

How do teams reach this level of commitment and dedication? In most cases there is someone who believes in the team, believes in what the team can accomplish and displays a level of enthusiasm that appears to come from an endless internal source of energy.

The building of the team takes time, but the rewards are certainly worth it. A strong team can meet most challenges and work to overcome any obstacle to success. If success is not achieved, the team works together to generate new ideas and form new plans, always looking at the opportunities and making revisions as necessary. Once a team has achieved a high level of performance, the leader must now create an environment that will keep the team together. As every team leader knows, each member is important and each has a specific job or role, but there are some who stand out among the rest. These are the MVPs (most valuable players)—the members of the team who have the talent to motivate, encourage and fire up the entire team's performance. These are people who set aside their egos and work to bring out the best in everyone else.

In the project environment and in the larger business environment, retaining key people is a priority among project managers and business managers. These people inspire others, offer new ideas, make things happen and can be relied upon to get the job done. They usually possess a variety of skills, are flexible, adaptable and can be placed in many roles.

These key players generate enormous value for the organization, and it would be worth the time and effort to develop a strategy to keep them. Part of that strategy is to create a sense of loyalty to the team and to the organization as a whole.

Retention should be viewed as a long-term effort. Key players may have much less loyalty to an organization that looks at them only when they are trying to protect company interests or when another organization has expressed an interest in an employee. What is needed is an environment in which the employee believes it's worth staying with the team or the organization. In the book *Retaining Your Best People* — a series of articles by several authors who have significant knowledge and experience in the subject, retention should become a core strategy.[1] I believe this applies to the enterprise and at the project level. Leaders need retention-related skills to keep their best people. These skills include the ability to attract talented people, provide meaningful performance feedback, observe warning signs of problems and potential dissention and establish a process for career advancement.

Leaders need to consider the interests of the team members, continuously work to understand what motivates the team and to ask the question: *What can we do to keep you?* A significant piece of advice from *Retaining Your Best People,* and something that all leaders should do on a regular basis, is to make sure you tell your team members, especially your best performers that you really treasure them, and that you count on them and have a desire to keep them happy and fulfilled. Reward them as often as you can and in as many ways as possible. The payoff here is loyalty and a willingness to remain with the team even when a talent poacher or headhunter is offering an enticing deal. Demonstrating sincere recognition and appreciation for the people on your team can actually be perceived as more important than a few extra dollars at another place of employment.

Keeping your best people is also related to cost. Losing a key player results in a need to bring in new talent, provide training, assimilate into the team and manage through the typical ramp-up time required. The period of team adjustment can take months depending on personalities, perceptions and the willingness of the team to accept the new player.

It is important to note that many studies about motivation indicate that compensation and monetary rewards are not on the top of the list of items that interest employees. Pay is certainly important, but most employees have other expectations. Today's managers and leaders should invest some time in learning more about what motivates generation X and Y employees. There should be an effort by the manager, project manager or business executive to determine what the non-monetary interests of the key players are. Team leaders should spend time learning about their team members, listening to their ideas and being available when a team member has an issue to discuss. The leader should also be visible in good times as well as when there are problems to address. The out-of-sight leader, the person who is only around to receive compliments that are intended for the team or stay out of the line-of-fire during crisis situations, will soon find themselves with a group of dissenters, who will look for an exit at the first opportunity.

A very basic leadership practice is to ensure that promises made are promises kept, and if action is committed, it must be performed. There is no faster way to lose key players than to fail to meet a commitment or renege on a promise. This sends a message that the individual is not important enough to follow through for and will place an indelible mark on your personal credibility.

Tips for Retaining Your Key Players

There are lots of methods and techniques for retaining key employees and team members. The following list is intended to be a springboard for more ideas. Consider your organization's strategic goals and consider the people you have in place who are attempting to meet those goals. Do they know where they stand regarding how you view them? Have you shown your appreciation? Do you know how they perceive you as a leader? Do you know what the warning signs are that a key player is considering opportunities in other organizations? When was the last time you said, "thanks"? When was the last time you praised a great idea?

Retaining Your MVPs and Key Players

Tom Peters wrote a book titled, *The Pursuit of Wow! Every Person's Guide to Topsy-Turvy Times*, and he said, create a *WOW project*.[2] If it's important enough for your organization to implement, then treat it that way. It starts with you, the project manager. If you are not excited about the project, don't expect anyone else to be. People connect with assignments that are important, interesting and value-adding. Your sincere enthusiasm is the main ingredient in retaining your people.

- **Avoid "Jerk-dom"** — The failure to acknowledge people who really deserve it or to offer insincere, lack luster praise, or to simply take credit yourself for the work of your team. Say thanks, offer words of support, show appreciation for good work and reward your key players as often as possible. People generally won't work for people who just don't care for them.

- **Communicate** — Keep your team members informed. Don't let them find out information from other sources that should have come from you. Ask questions and listen to suggestions. Always follow up when you make a commitment or accept and idea.
- **Stay visible** — Team members feel more confident when they know the leader is available for support.
- **Maintain a positive presence and attitude** — Smile. It's contagious!
- **Provide open and honest feedback** — How you deliver criticism is crucial.
- **Provide challenges and offer encouragement and confidence** — People need to stretch a little to help them see just how far they can go. Most will step up to the challenge, and will appreciate your trust.
- **Minimize your supervision** — Provide a sense of autonomy. Freedom is a major motivator and builds trust on both sides.
- **Ask for feedback and keep an open mind** — You may not like some of the feedback you receive from your team, but how you react to it will definitely impact your team. If you have established a trusting and open environment, there should be fewer surprises.
- **Retention is as important as recruiting** — Perhaps, retention is even more important due to the amount of time and training you have invested in your team. Create a strategy that will keep people interested in the project and/or the organization. Develop plans that will help them to improve their performance. Loyal teams will make a difference during tough times. There will generally be a willingness to work for less or to do more when necessary, if the leadership has invested the time and effort and created a culture of appreciation.

Your Personal Leadership Action Register

Consider the team or teams you are working with today. Can you determine the level of loyalty that exists? Who are your MVPs? Do you treat some team members more favorably than others? Do you have an acknowledgement plan? Use this page to further develop a plan for your own personal growth as a leader. Each chapter contains many references and sources of information. Use these references and any personal notes you have documented to assist you in designing a plan that will achieve your leadership goals. Make a note of insights, key learning points, personal recommendations, areas for review, books to read, self-development plans and topics of interest you would like to research.

_____

_____

_____

_____

_____

_____

_____

_____

_____

_____

_____

_____

_____

_____

_____

_____

_____

_____

_____

_____

Personal Leadership Activities
Figure 17.1

Action Item	Target Date for Completion
Assess my team's overall synergy. Develop plans to ensure everyone is well connected and has a sense of being appreciated	
Conduct informal feedback sessions with team members and identify issues or areas where I can personally make improvements	

18 Managing Your Leadership Role

> "I am a man of fixed and unbending principles, the first of which is to be flexible at all times."
> — Everett Dirksen

All leaders, regardless of style or skills, should have a personal management and maintenance plan. Just like a vehicle needs maintenance every 10,000 miles, a machine needs care and attention to keep it running smoothly, or a project needs a review at the end of each phase, leaders need some type of leadership maintenance check. Even if things appear to be going well, we schedule check-ups for our cars, equipment we use and even our own bodies: So why not schedule a *Leadership Review*? If your project is progressing smoothly and your team is working well together, take some time to find out why things are doing so well. If things were going poorly, you can be sure that there would be inquiries, reviews, audits and lots of questions. Your leadership skills have a lot to do with the success of your project and the ability of the team to work together. It is more beneficial to know what works than to know what doesn't work.

In a scene from the movie *Apollo 13*, the flight team struggles to deal with the situation that has been developing and is acting erratically, without any visible sense of cohesion. The flight director, Gene Kranz, must deal with the explosion aboard the space craft and the plight of the astronauts. He masterfully directs his command center team to regain their focus by asking them to think in terms of status. He needed to know what was working to help him assess the situation and determine a course of action. Understanding what is working and concentrating on the actions, and behaviors that make things work will help to reduce the negativity that distracts people and creates problems.

In a seminar I attended several years ago, the speaker emphasized the need to focus on the positive behaviors of people in an organization or on a team. Constantly looking at the negatives increases the awareness of the negatives and results in more of those negatives. People will actually focus on and give more attention to the negative behaviors and actions than what really needs to be acted upon. This concentrated focus on what went wrong, who failed to deliver, who should be punished and what can't be done is an undesirable situation. Constantly bringing up problem areas, highlighting poor performance and always looking to blame someone would certainly undermine the capabilities of even the strongest team members. I don't know many coaches who spend their time discouraging their team by pointing to failure after failure. Teams become winners by building their confidence and skills. Focusing on positive behaviors results in more teamwork and productivity, higher morale and increased motivation.

You can see this coaching approach in action in the movie *Miracle*, about the 1980 U.S. Olympic Men's Hockey Team. The movie provides an excellent view of a coach's determination to build a team that believes in itself. The coach sees the potential of the team, internalizes that belief and creates a strategy that initially seems harsh, but achieves its goals and much more effectively.

Recharging the Leader

It takes a lot of energy to be a leader. Occasionally, a leader needs a little rest to recharge, look back, look ahead and look around. Strong leaders who are passionate about their organizations, teams or goals occasionally go just a step too far and start running on borrowed energy. This energy reserve will eventually run out and when that happens, the machine can break down. Before breakdown occurs, it makes sense to have a leadership maintenance plan or a leadership recharging process in place to keep the team going and to give them a feeling of stability. Just like a business has a disaster recovery and business continuity plan, every leader needs a leadership recovery and continuity plan. Here are a few thoughts and ideas that can keep your leadership engine running smoothly and effectively.

1. Display enthusiasm — Show your team that you really enjoy working with them. Enthusiasm is contagious, and you will find that it increases teamwork and reduces your personal stress by emphasizing the positives.

2. Give a sense of urgency — Ensure that your team is aware of the importance of the project, and how they are needed to make it successful. This will help to reduce unproductivity, such as time spent supervising. It will give you a better opportunity to observe the team in action.

3. Spend time with your team — Ask questions, recognize good performance and most importantly, listen to their suggestions. Make sure you respond to their suggestions even if you decide not to use them. Leaders who connect with their teams will spend less energy managing them.

4. Communicate — A well-informed team reduces the need for meetings and provides more time to accomplish tasks. Failure to communicate effectively creates stress for both sides and results in significant time spent clarifying and explaining.

5. Check your power level — What types of personal power are you using? Is it reward, penalty, formal, referent or expert? Maybe yours is a combination of all types. Evaluate how you use power to get things done. Power doesn't have to be at full blast all of the time. Use your internal power adjustment controls and regulate how you use power—running at maximum will only wear you down.

6. Schedule a leadership review — There are many tools available to obtain feedback about your leadership effectiveness, from a 360-degree feedback process to a one-on-one discussion. Sometimes we behave in a manner that causes problems and uneasiness among our team, but since there is no obvious indication that a problem exists, we continue to act the same way. We need feedback to obtain information about how our projects are doing and how we, as leaders, are being perceived.

7. Take a break — Give authority to someone else every once in a while. Show your trust and respect. Take a few days off. Exercise a little. Practice healthful leadership by taking care of yourself as well as the team. The team needs you, so don't push too far. Remember what Clint Eastwood said in the movie Magnum Force: "A man's got to know his limitations."[1] To be more focused on the point, a project manager's got to know his or her limitations!

Take some time and check your leadership power supply. Develop a plan to keep yourself charged up and build in some recharge time. Don't burn out your team, either. Build some enjoyment into your project. As Tom Peters said, make your project a Wow! project.[2] People should look at your project and your team and say, "Wow, I wish I was a part of that team!" Or, just stare in amazement at what you have accomplished!

Your Personal Leadership Action Register

Continue to develop a plan for your personal growth as a leader. Each chapter contains many references, sources of information and ideas intended to inspire.

Use these references and any personal notes you have documented to assist you in designing a plan that will achieve your leadership goals.

Make a note of insights, key learning points, personal recommendations, areas for review, books to read, self-development plans and topics of interest you would like to research. Each chapter was written with the intention that the thoughts and ideas will trigger your mind to stretch, consider new ways of accomplishing your goals and focus on the constant reinvention of *you*.

_____
_____
_____
_____
_____
_____
_____
_____
_____
_____
_____
_____
_____
_____
_____
_____
_____
_____
_____
_____
_____
_____
_____
_____

Personal Leadership Activities
Figure 18.1

Action Item	Target Date for Completion
List the reasons why your project is a *Wow! Project*	
Ask your team to explain why they are proud to work together on the project	
Schedule acknowledgments for your team members	

19 Creating Your Personal Leadership Checklist

"The only safe ship in a storm is leadership."
— Faye Wattleton

"Whoever is providing leadership needs to be as fresh and thoughtful and reflective as possible to make the very best fight."
— Faye Wattleton

There are probably hundreds of ways to assess your personal leadership qualities. You can simply ask someone for feedback, participate in a 360-degree feedback process or just look at the results that your team is producing. Whatever method you use, chances are you will find some areas for improvement. Leaders should be continuously looking for areas where they can improve how they work with people, lead teams and influence their organizations. Improvement should be part of every leader's personal plan (for example, finding new ways of doing something, selecting and working with a mentor, developing a better method of team motivation, learning something that is outside of your area of expertise, reading a book about leadership or scheduling a few informal meetings with employees or business associates).

If you ask around your organization or within your personal network of contacts, you will find that many people define leadership in the same way—traits like good communicator, easy to work with, has a vision, is organized and more. But these are qualities that are on the surface. We need to dig a little deeper to see what it takes to be a truly effective leader. It can be a little difficult to do this without a framework to start from.

Every organization will define leadership somewhat differently based on organizational culture, type of business, geographic location and other factors, but I believe that there are some common elements below the surface that we can build on. The following table is a Leadership Checklist to help get you started. Review each item. I think you will find that most of the items listed would be included in any organization's list of leadership qualities.

A LEADERSHIP CHECKLIST
FIGURE 19.1

STRATEGIC PLANNING	Clearly Demonstrated	Needs Improvement	Not Demonstrated
1. Implements and achieves results that support the business's strategic goals and direction			
2. Sets and meets commitments			
3. Understands and manages the interdependencies of the business units and/or functional groups within the organization			
4. Understands the critical success factors and Key Performance Indicators that drive the organization and create a sustainable future			

STRATEGIC LEADERSHIP	Clearly Demonstrated	Needs Improvement	Not Demonstrated
5. Develops creative approaches to resolve issues and achieve objectives			
6. Strives to be innovative. Offers new ideas and alternatives to meet business needs			
7. Understands the key business issues affecting the organization and communicates those issues effectively			
8. Comprehends the larger picture and sees the corporate point of view			
9. Pursues quality and strives for continuous improvement			
10. Understands and applies systems thinking to ensure that each element of the organization is clearly considered and represented			
11. Demonstrates the ability to make difficult decisions that are in the best interest of the organization and deal with the consequences of those decisions			

Team Building	Clearly Demonstrated	Needs Improvement	Not Demonstrated
12. Develops strong working relationships with peers and subordinates			
13. Resolves conflicts through a collaborative, win-win approach whenever possible			
14. Understands the escalation protocol and resolves issues at the appropriate management level. Does not unnecessarily involve upper management in conflict resolution			

MOTIVATES THE TEAM AND THE ORGANIZATION	Clearly Demonstrated	Needs Improvement	Not Demonstrated
15. Demonstrates commitment to the organization's goals and vision through words and actions			
16. Demonstrates leadership by example and helps to develop aspiring leaders			
17. Actively listens to subordinates and associates to obtain new ideas			.
18. Provides opportunities for growth among the team through professional development, coaching, and mentoring			
19. Encourages risk taking, provides constructive feedback after a mistake is made, and deflects recognition to the team upon completion of objectives			

This list can be further developed to be more comprehensive but it provides a good framework to create a checklist of your own. Before you start the list, take some time and ask your co-workers and associates the following questions:

- Have you ever worked for a person who you thought was a truly effective leader?
- What was it about that person that impressed you?
- Would you work for that person again and why?
- What trait or characteristic of that person made the most significant impact on your career or affected the way you work with other people?

You don't necessarily need a name; just find out what people believe are the characteristics of a great leader, what leaders do to demonstrate their qualities and abilities and why people follow them. I believe the checklist will be relatively easy to create. It will be well worth the time and will help you to enhance your existing leadership capabilities, while keeping you on that always-evolving track toward truly exceptional leadership.

Your Personal Leadership Action Register

Leadership is a continuous journey. You never actually arrive at a leadership summit. There is always something new to learn, an experience you haven't had and a new horizon in the distance.

Continue to develop a plan for your own personal growth as a leader. Each chapter contains many references and sources of information. Use these references and any personal notes you have documented to assist you in designing a plan that will achieve your leadership goals.

Make a note of insights, key learning points, personal recommendations, areas for review, books to read, self-development plans and topics of interest you would like to research.

_____
_____
_____
_____
_____
_____
_____
_____
_____
_____
_____
_____
_____
_____
_____
_____
_____
_____
_____
_____

Personal Leadership Activities
Figure 19.2

Action Item	Target Date for Completion
Review the leadership checklist and add additional items that are related to my areas of responsibility	
Review my methods of motivation and identify new ways to keep the team enthusiastic	

20 The Importance of Connective Leadership

> "You must unite your constituents around a common cause and connect with them as human beings."
> — James Kouzes and Barry Posner

You may have noticed from previous chapters that leadership can be defined in many different ways. There is no one truly universal definition of leadership. The definition will vary depending on who you are, your age, where you live, your family background, your education, where you work, your heritage, your personal values and many more areas of influence. The type of leadership style that you demonstrate to others also has a lot to do with your personal values and varies depending on the situation you find yourself in at any particular time.

Positive Leadership focuses on the needs of the organization and the people who carry out the tasks to achieve the objectives of the organization. It doesn't mean being soft and avoiding tough decisions or addressing issues that are comfortable for everyone. It means commitment to the organization and its employees. It means placing the organization above personal interests and making the right decisions. Sometimes these decisions will not be popular. Decisions made by leaders are often based on information that is not always available to those who will be affected by the decision. This may result in some resistance because of an inability to see the bigger picture. But with the proper amount of useful, informative communication, sincere effort to identify alternatives and, if possible, programs that will mitigate any hardships or significant changes to employees, the benefits of Positive Leadership will be recognized and respected.

There is no question that organizations, regardless of size or discipline, need strong leaders who are willing to make decisions and accept responsibility for their actions. These are people with vision, commitment and the ability to influence their constituents to bring about results. The need for strong leadership applies to project management as well. It is essential for project managers to accept that they have been assigned to a leadership position and they must display the characteristics of Positive Leadership.

Building Positive Leadership

The leaders of today and tomorrow should consider the following key factors if they expect to be successful:

- Take care of your team. Without your team, nothing can be accomplished.
- Take care of the people who perform the work that must be done every day. Acknowledgment, encouragement and appreciation are essential for effective leadership.
- Communicate regularly. Don't distance yourself from the very people you need to achieve desired objectives and success.
- Respect your team members and employees.
- Show firmness but be fair and willing to listen to suggestions.
- Demonstrate integrity. Leaders set the example.
- Listen more.
- Build trust by keeping your commitments.

Organizational or team success depends on a simple principle: Take care of the inside — your team — and the outside will shine brightly. Your leadership capabilities and your ability to achieve results are displayed through the actions and attitudes of your team. Strong, Positive Leadership will inspire not only your team members but the people who are watching as you lead. It's this personal mastery that makes the person a true leader.

CONNECTIVE LEADERSHIP

Connective leadership is a type of leadership that directs energy toward bringing together diverse organizations or conflicting groups that exist in an interdependent environment.[1] The project environment is certainly interdependent and an established and well-connected team with a common set of objectives is truly desirable. Project managers are quite aware that without a solid, highly performing and dedicated team, meeting the expectations of clients and key stakeholders would be basically impossible. A team that is well-connected within itself and with the leader creates the foundation for success.

The most successful project managers understand the concept of interdependence in the project environment.

- Interdependence is driven by a systems-thinking approach to achieving objectives and by the rapid changes in technology. Systems-thinking focuses on the bigger picture and how parts come together to create the whole. Technology connects everyone. It drives people toward greater levels of collaboration, new alliances and new networks.
- Interdependence creates the need to develop joint visions, to focus on mutual problems, establish common goals and create a feeling of confidence, strength and unity.

Considering the many deliverables of most projects and the interactions of multiple functional entities, managing these interdependencies is the key to connective leadership. The concept of connective leadership was introduced by Jean Lipman-Blumen in her book, *Connective Leadership: Managing in a Changing World*, and has been expanded upon by the Connective Leadership Institute. It involves three styles of leadership: direct, relational and instrumental.[2]

- The direct style is competitive and focuses on power. This type of leader assumes credit for work that is accomplished.
- The relational style supports a collaborative approach to accomplishing objectives and is more group-centered.

- The instrumental style is entrusting, social and personal, and goes beyond collaboration to create a high degree of unity and togetherness to achieve the organization's goals.

The focus of this chapter is directed at instrumental leadership, also referred to as transformational leadership. An instrumental leader is an expert at uniting people, teams or organizations and has a natural ability to influence others and win them over to join a specific cause. A transformational leader has the ability to motivate a team, maintain high morale and achieve superior levels of organizational performance. I have therefore combined these two similar leadership styles, as I believe that the application of these styles is instrumental to team, organizational and personal success. The Project Management Institute (PMI®) *A Guide to the Project Management Body of Knowledge (PMBOK® Guide)* defines leadership as follows:

- establishing direction - developing a vision of the future and the strategies to achieve that vision
- aligning people - communicating by words and deeds
- motivating and inspiring - energizing and helping people to overcome barriers to change[3]

Leadership involves much more than the listed items but in general, these bullets support what most people will accept as a definition of leadership. There are, however, some additional aspects of leadership that should be considered in order to become a truly instrumental leader.

- People respond to strong leadership and individuals who set a clear course of action and direction.
- The power of well-defined and clearly demonstrated leadership cannot be underestimated. History has shown us how leadership can change the world or a country. Powerful leadership in business transforms small or struggling companies into trendsetting juggernauts.
- Leadership includes the ability to influence behavior at the individual and organizational level, the ability to adapt to change and to cause constructive change, the ability to

overcome resistance to change and the ability to inspire people to do things they would not otherwise do.

Instrumental leadership is demonstrated through words as well as actions. Leaders must be able to speak leadership, using words that inspire, build trust and truly indicate commitment. In the book *The Leadership Challenge*, Kouzes and Posner's research indicates that there are four characteristics of words commonly used by leaders:[4]

- Realistic words portray tangible and concrete objects. We use realistic words to describe project deliverables and help people to visualize what is intended to be accomplished. Examples of realistic words are infrastructure, bridge, building and space station.
- Optimistic words express hope and possibilities. As a project manager, you must continuously display a positive attitude and be a source of strength. Project management is not about hoping that things happen - it's about belief in the team, encouraging people to think in terms of opportunities and instilling a belief that problems can be solved. Examples of optimistic words are bright, positive and confident.
- Activity words show motion. Focus on getting things done by assigning responsibility for activities that are clearly defined, necessary and can be accomplished. Intentionally explain your expectations about what your team should accomplish and how they should perform their activities. Examples of activity word are build, climb, jump, stretch, reach and overtake.
- Certainty words express assuredness. As project managers, we must remain confident in ourselves and our teams. Certainty words reflect on realistic outcomes and indicate the belief that people can accomplish the goals and objectives that have been established. Examples of certainty words are will, able, definite, conviction, fact and reality.

What Instrumental Leaders Know

Some people believe that leadership skills are acquired during conception and birth (born leaders). Others believe that leadership skills are acquired and developed over time through education, coaching and mentoring. I am sure that both views can be argued successfully. In either case, the effective leader relies on intuition as some part of the success equation. The following list, adapted from *The Leadership Challenge*, provides us with some additional leadership nuggets that experienced leaders have learned and practiced:

- The truly instrumental leader can make the intangible image of the future tangible and concrete. As project managers, it is imperative that we communicate effectively and use our skills to help our teams paint a mental picture of how the project will turn out. We must become masters at creating a vision. It is important to remove fuzzy perceptions and crystallize the goals and objectives of the project.
- Effective leaders offer positive and optimistic predictions that the dream or vision will be realized. Focus on the success factors that make sense and instill a belief that objectives will be achieved, but be prepared for challenges and inevitable change.
- Effective leaders demonstrate confidence. They also know when goals cannot be achieved. Remain realistic and ensure that goals remain grounded. We want our teams to believe that, as leaders, we know when to change direction or change a strategy.
- Effective leaders propel the mission of the project or the organization. Combine energy and motion and create an unstoppable force. Project leaders are the energizers and provide a source of strength for the project team. True leaders also realize that an occasional recharge will be required. Use the talents of the team, challenge their abilities and encourage energy transfers between team members to ensure that everyone is working together

but take time occasionally to reflect on what has been accomplished and offer some sincere acknowledgments.

Leadership encompasses much more than most of us had imagined when we began our leadership journey and it is displayed in numerous forms and styles. There is no one-size-fits-all type of leadership, but we need to adapt to a leadership style that fits us well and will enable us to accomplish our own personal goals and make a difference in our respective organizations.

Bringing all of the ideas and concepts together, I have modified the term connective leadership. To me, it is the ability to take the integrity, energy and commitment of the leader, instill trust within the team and tap into the individual strengths of the team members, to create a willingness to achieve the objectives of the project or the organization. Connective leadership is just what it suggests:

- Giving your project team a foundation to develop a true and undeniable belief that the leader and team are connected through shared goals.
- Clearly understanding your personal values, adapting them as needed and then communicating your personal commitment to the team.
- Building on the team's strengths, talents and abilities to produce world class performance.
- Establishing a core set of team values that are consistently demonstrated.
- Creating an environment where extraordinary results are achieved through innovation and collaboration.
- Establishing mutual trust and respect.
- Establishing and communicating a vision that is inspiring, attainable, accepted and owned by the entire project team.

Connecting the Energy

I couldn't find the right word or phrase that would capture the result of a well-connected team so I combined a few words and created the term "connectic energy," which is derived from

Kinetic – from the Greek word *kinetikos*; of or relating to the motion of material bodies and the forces and energy associated therewith.[5]

Energy – from the Greek word *energeia*; the capacity of acting or being active, natural power vigorously exerted.[6]

Kinetic Energy – energy associated with motion.[7] Combining these words, I've defined "connectic energy" as:

> "The sustained energy experienced through a continuous movement forward; refueled by communication, lessons learned, teamwork, sharing of experiences and visionary leadership."

Today's project managers must be effective, connective leaders who fully understand the power of leadership. Just like quality improvement, leadership is a journey, not a destination. Similar to risk management, it is needed regardless of the type of project. Leadership is also part of the system of project management and like requirements for your project, it can be difficult to define and subject to change.

The best advice I can give about leadership is to continue learning about it. Look for opportunities to improve your skills whenever you can. Obtain feedback often and embrace that feedback. Learn from your experiences, adapt to change and use the strengths of your team. Your team will appreciate your ability to connect with them and the rewards will be self-evident.

Your Personal Leadership Action Register

Consider your personal leadership style. Does it lean more to the "dark side" or the positive side? Are you a connective leader? Are you generating connectic energy?

Develop a plan for your own personal growth as a leader. Each chapter contains references and sources of information. Use these references and any personal notes you have documented to assist you in designing a plan that will achieve your leadership goals.

Make a note of insights, key learning points, personal recommendations, areas for review, books to read, self-development plans and topics of interest you would like to research.

Personal Leadership Activities
Figure 20.1

Action Item	Target Date for Completion
Define my positive leadership characteristics	
Define my leadership "dark side"	
Develop a plan that will strengthen my positive side and transfer the power of the "dark side" to a more productive approach	

21 In Pursuit of Wow! Leadership

"A leader must have the courage to act against an expert's advice."
— James Callaghan

"There's nothing more demoralizing than a leader who can't clearly articulate why we're doing what we're doing."
— James Kouzes and Barry Posner

"Leaders can conceive and articulate goals that lift people out of their petty preoccupations and unite them in pursuit of objectives worthy of their best efforts."
— John Gardner

If asked the question: "Who comes to mind when you think about great leadership?" We would probably respond with hundreds of names. Even though there is a generally accepted list of effective leadership traits and characteristics, we each have our own personal definition and perception of effective leadership. "Managers do things right and leaders do the right things," is a familiar example. We expect leaders to make changes, improve our lives, increase profit, motivate the work force, communicate good and bad news, make tough decisions, keep us safe and know how to solve every problem and answer every question. Actually, the truly effective leader may not know the answer to every problem but will know who to contact to work through the issues or how to go about finding the answers. Yes, leaders should have a vision, effective communications skills and all of those traits associated with the word "leader," but what is much more important is the ability to motivate a team or an organization to do great things. When asked about their projects, their place of employment or the organization that they belong to, team members or employees should talk about their projects or their organizations from the Wow! perspective. This means speaking with enthusiasm. The listener should hear a noticeable tone and feel a sincerity that comes from the heart with true and honest pride. Have you ever listened to someone tell you about something they are truly passionate about? Maybe it's a new car or a garden or a completed weekend home project. Maybe you heard an artist who just completed his or her latest work, exclaiming with a sense of accomplishment. They speak with an intensity and deep sense of emotion. They are communicating to you in such a way that you feel compelled to respond with a simple yet powerful statement—"Wow!"

Now let's apply the Wow! perspective to the projects you are working on. Do you consider them Wow! projects? Do your team members express pride and enthusiasm when discussing the projects with other people in the organization? Do you inspire your team through your own enthusiasm? Do you motivate the team through high energy and a real sense of ownership? If not, how can you expect your team to respond with anything more than mediocrity?

The "wow factor" is about creating an environment that helps people understand the importance of the project you are assigned to. It means making sure that others see your project as important, regardless of size or complexity. When speaking about your project, the response from your audience, whether it's one person or twenty, should always be, "Wow! That's a great project!" (There will be exceptions, I know, but let's look at our projects from a positive viewpoint to match the context.) You won't get that response if you display a look of indifference or boredom while discussing your project. Remember, body language and other non-verbal communications are about 58 percent of our message.[1] We, as project managers, must show our teams that the project is important and therefore we must believe that it's important. Leaders are stewards of the organization's resources and if we follow the general principles of project management, the projects selected should be considered as important, necessary and supporting the overall strategic objectives of the organization. If that's the case, our next step is to ensure the project is considered a Wow! project by all of our key stakeholders.

Tom Peters and his book *The Pursuit of Wow! Every Person's Guide to Topsy-Turvy Times,* are the inspiration for this chapter. The book offers suggestions that help to catapult imaginations and have people become not just good managers and leaders, but Wow!ers. What we need in today's demanding project management environment are more project Wow!ers[2] leaders who will inspire, motivate and guide their teams to success after success.

Become a Leader of Wow!

As a project manager and leader, part of your responsibility is to instill within your team the desire to accomplish the project objectives - not because it's their job but because they believe it's the right thing to do, because they believe it's important to the success of the organization, and because it's important to each of them individually.

Here are a few things you can do to become a project Wow!er:

- Maintain a high level of enthusiasm for your project.
- Be careful not to criticize or complain about your project or team to other people. It will get back to your team.
- Send thank you notes. They are very powerful and appreciated.
- Recognize your team often.
- Don't be punishment averse. Address non-performers and people who are out of line.
- Be there — don't be invisible to your team.
- Stand behind your team in rough times and periods of stress. Manage your own stress but show your team that you are human. Understand and develop your emotional

intelligence.
- Watch out for the little stuff. Small things can do great damage over time. Emphasize the need for your team to focus on the details — you focus on the big picture.
- Celebrate small wins. Projects are lots of small wins so make sure you take time to emphasize them.
- Network like crazy — talk to people, get ideas, promote your project.
- Have a power breakfast or lunch — don't eat alone. Use this time to market your project, yourself or your team.
- Study relentlessly — I particularly like this one. Keep learning. Find out more about your clients and the people you work with (birthdays, special events). Find out about their needs and key issues. Be prepared!

Your commitment to the project is one of the key ingredients to success and your team will be able to tell just how committed you are. As Tom Peters says in his book, "People can smell emotional commitment from a mile away!"[3] Look closely at your projects. Do you have a Wow! project? Can you make it a Wow! project? It's up to you!

Your Personal Leadership Action Register

Leadership, in part, is creating that Wow! feeling among your team members. Do you have the right attitude and level of enthusiasm to inspire your team to achieve the wow factor? Develop a plan for your own personal growth as a leader. Each chapter contains many references and sources of information. Use these references and any personal notes you have documented to assist you in designing a plan that will achieve your leadership goals.

Make a note of insights, key learning points, personal recommendations, areas for review, books to read, self-development plans and topics of interest you would like to research.

Personal Leadership Activities
Figure 21.1

Action Item	Target Date for Completion
Connect with leaders from other organizations	
Discuss the challenges of being in a leadership position	
Ask other leaders what they do when they are with a situation that has never been experienced before	

22 When Leaders Need Leadership

"The key to successful leadership today is influence, not authority."
— Kenneth Blanchard

There should be no doubt in anyone's mind that accepting a position as a project manager also means accepting the responsibilities of a leader. The person accepting the assignment must be aware of the expectations associated with the position and the demands at the personal and professional levels. Of course, the type of project, the company, the organizational structure and other factors impact the role of the project manager but there will always be some element of leadership to the position.

We have previously defined leadership as "establishing direction, aligning people, motivating and inspiring people to overcome political, bureaucratic and resource barriers."[1] It falls under the heading of Key Management Skills and we would all like to believe that leaders possess the skills needed to achieve success for the team. People expect leadership from leaders. Leaders set the pace — they keep things moving and they become a source of energy. A strong leader creates a feeling of confidence among project team members and keeps the team working together, especially through difficult times. People don't expect to see a leader falter in any way. Leaders are looked upon as go-to people with solutions to every problem.

So how do so many leaders maintain that image of self-control, calmness and seemingly unlimited strength? I'm not sure if there is any one answer to that question but I believe it has a lot to do with the statement made by Clint Eastwood in the movie *Magnum Force*: "A man's got to know his limitations."[2] (That quote is one of my favorites and I use it often.) Sometimes people in leadership positions push a little too hard, take on more than they should, assume other people's burdens or make promises that they cannot keep. This may result in a loss of credibility and trust and, in worst cases, even job termination. Everyone has limitations, no one is infallible and everyone makes mistakes. Understanding your limitations does not mean putting on the brakes. It means rethinking how to get things done and knowing when to ask for help.

If you observe successful leaders, you will likely notice they surround themselves with incredibly competent people, who are leaders themselves. These are people who leaders can trust, discuss sensitive issues with and ask for advice. Many leaders have mentors, who act as sounding boards to help them think through problems and decisions. I read a statement by Bill Cosby that really has a good message for leaders. Cosby said, "I don't know what the key to success is but the key to failure is trying to please everyone." I believe that effective leaders, even if they have never heard that quote, make it a point to avoid failure by not trying to please everyone. Leadership is about accepting responsibility for decisions and making decisions that may be very unpopular. Leaders know their limitations or the boundaries they must work within. They have a vision, a mission and a desire to achieve their objectives, and they find ways to achieve them.

Here's where the real leadership skills kick in. These skills include enabling/empowering others, communicating goals clearly, listening, maintaining a level of flexibility, influencing others and innovating. If there were a set of keys to success for leaders, I am sure a major component would be the ability to enable others to reach their potential. Leaders achieve success by providing direction and allowing others to act. When things become difficult, the leader looks for leadership from the team. This is a true strength because leaders know the value their team provides and regardless of leadership style, their success depends on the team's collective knowledge and abilities. Strong leaders gain from their teams' strengths and know when to ask for help. Asking for help isn't a sign of weakness - it's a sign of respect for true leadership.

Your Personal Leadership Action Register

Leaders gain experience from other leaders. They obtain knowledge and make decisions based on input from several sources. It is important to create strong relationships with knowledgeable people who are a source of wisdom and reason.

Develop a plan for your own personal growth as a leader. Each chapter contains many references and sources of information. Use these references and any personal notes you have documented to assist you in designing a plan that will achieve your leadership goals.

Make a note of insights, key learning points, personal recommendations, areas for review, books to read, self-development plans and topics of interest you would like to research.

Personal Leadership Activities
Figure 22.1

Action Item	Target Date for Completion
Connect with leaders from other organizations. Discuss the challenges of being in a leadership position. Ask other leaders what they do when they are faced with a situation that has never been experienced before	

23 Encouraging Innovation

"The function of leadership is to produce more leaders, not more followers."
— Ralph Nader

"Get a good idea and stay with it. Dog it, and work at it until it's done right."
— Walt Disney

"Happiness lies in the joy of achievement and the thrill of creative effort."
— Franklin D. Roosevelt

Q*WERTYUIOP.* Do you recognize this configuration of letters? You see them every day when you look at your computer keyboard. This is the top row of letters on a standard computer keyboard. You have also seen them on word processors and yes, typewriters (although for many of you, typewriters and vinyl records share a similar place in history—near extinction). Whether you have used a typewriter or are now using a computer keyboard, we generally take this configuration for granted and don't give much thought as to why the letters are arranged this way. It's a standard set-up and regardless of make or model of computer, the keyboards are basically the same. Surprisingly enough, there's a connection between these letters and innovation and creativity.

In the 1870s, the leading manufacturer of typewriters, Sholes & Co., was faced with a challenge. Operators using their typewriters complained that the keys would stick together if they typed too fast. This occurred because the arms connected to the keys, designed to strike the paper with the chosen letter, would jam together and require the operator to disengage them by hand. This was a big problem for the user and an even bigger problem for the engineers who designed the machine. Top management needed a solution and the engineers had difficulty finding one that worked. There was much discussion until someone asked, "What if we slowed the operators down?" The letters were rearranged to place the most frequently used letters in positions that would use the weakest fingers to depress them. This logic was used to create the new keyboard and solved the problem of sticking keys. This is a great example of innovative thinking and the idea has endured through advances in technology.

Today there are no mechanical keys or major arms on our computers and smart phones that can stick but the same logic for the letter arrangement remains in use, even though there are new configurations that could increase operator speed. The point is, once a rule or a method has been put in place and is followed for a long period of time, it becomes a norm and it is very difficult to eliminate, even when the original reason for the rule no longer exists. Author Roger von Oech refers to this as the "Aslan Phenomenon"— the following of an obsolete rule.[1]

The Aslan Phenomenon explained: Roger von Oech, author of *A Whack on the Side of the Head: How to Unlock Your Mind for Innovation*, routinely ran every day and at the end of his run he would stop to cool down. He picked a spot where there was a big golden retriever named Aslan. He thought it was a good spot to stop and would pet the dog and cool down. As a rule, he would always end his run at the spot where the dog was. The owner eventually moved, taking Aslan with him, but von Oech would continue to end his run at this spot even though Aslan was no longer there.[2]

This created what von Oech describes as the Aslan Phenomenon.

1. We make rules based on reasons that make a lot of sense.
2. We follow these rules.
3. Time passes and things change.

4. The original reasons for the generation of these rules no longer exist but because these rules are still in place, we continue to follow them.³

Project managers face new situations every day and occasionally rules have to be questioned. Creative thinking is initiated when rules and the status quo are challenged, and today's demanding project and business environments require new ideas, better tools, methods and fast thinking. This means that today's project managers must possess an innovative quality and the ability to influence and encourage their teams to seek creative solutions to new and more complex project situations.

An ad placed by Microsoft in a popular magazine stated that the future success of any business depends on its next generation of leaders. We can apply this same thinking to project management. We need project leaders who are innovative and will take the profession to higher and higher levels of performance and value. If you think about it, managing a project is actually doing something that hasn't been done before. Yes, projects that you are currently assigned to may be similar to projects that you or your associates have done in the past but as we know from many project management source materials, projects are unique. When doing something new or unique, there will be new obstacles to overcome, new ideas to consider and some creative genius that must be brought to the table. New ideas drive the business world forward and we need new ideas to drive projects toward success. New ideas will also encourage project team members to exercise their creative abilities.

We need methods, procedures and standards to avoid chaos but we don't live in a "one-project-methodology-fits-all" environment. What we need is fresh thinking for new projects. Lessons learned are important and can help to keep us out of trouble but we should also be asking the "what if" questions (particularly important when reviewing a completed phase or project), and looking for better ways to achieve our goals. If a task was executed very well, ask how it can be done even better the next time—for example, "This worked great, but what if we changed the sequence?" If a task is not completed successfully, ask questions like, "What if we tried a different approach?" Even if a project doesn't work out as planned, there are new ideas just waiting to emerge. Think of failed projects or failed attempts as some type of a project phoenix. Imagine if the project manager in *The Flight of the Phoenix*, in which survivors of a plane crash in the Gobi Desert work together to build a new plane, only saw the wreckage. Surely the outcome would be very different. Look for opportunity in any situation—especially the difficult ones. Though it may not be obvious, some creative thought and imagination will help you find what you need.

Innovation is essential for project success. Sometimes new ideas are just beyond our line of sight and we need the team to help us see beyond the boundaries and limitations that we've set. Encourage your teams to be creative, question the rules occasionally and promote internal, informal discussions and dialogue. Many great ideas have been launched through informal meetings where people felt relaxed and allowed their minds to work without stress.

Provide an environment that celebrates successes and capitalizes on mistakes. Mistakes can be expected, so rather than creating fear of making a mistake, create an environment where people think about how to avoid problems but can still take risks that allow for growth through the knowledge of experience. Success breeds more of the same and with the right guidance, even mistakes can lead to new thinking and improved ways of getting things done. Project leaders should consider themselves to be creativity stimulators and enablers. Challenge your team to think of options and alternatives, remove inhibitors that block creativity and be supportive even when things don't work out. Make it a point to reward your team members when something goes well and always keep your team informed.

One last thought, many people think that they just aren't creative but the fact is, everyone is creative to some extent. It's leadership that makes the breakthroughs possible. Work with your teams and engage them. Show your appreciation for their willingness to meet challenges head-on and ensure that they know their work is valued. Provide an environment that encourages and rewards creative solutions. Your organization will truly benefit from the creative energy that is just waiting to be unleashed.

Your Personal Leadership Action Register

Creativity and innovation are essential for any organization to survive. Leaders should encourage team members and employees to continually look for the next best thing. There are numerous tools, techniques and activities that can help to develop the creative talents of your organization.

Develop a plan for your own personal growth as a leader. Each chapter contains many references and sources of information. Use these references and any personal notes you have documented to assist you in designing a plan that will achieve your leadership goals.

Make a note of insights, key learning points, personal recommendations, areas for review, books to read, self-development plans and topics of interest you would like to research.

Personal Leadership Activities
Figure 23.1

Action Item	Target Date for Completion
Read about techniques that can improve your team's ability to solve problems	
Schedule a team activity that is enjoyable and will encourage creative thinking	

24 Common Sense Project Leadership

"Leaders are more powerful role models when they learn than when they teach."
— Rosabeth Moss Kanter

When someone mentions the phrase "common sense," I immediately think of something that Dr. Steven Covey, author of *The 7 Habits of Highly Effective People*, said: "Common sense is not always common practice."[1] I have also heard many people say that project management is nothing more than organized common sense. Maybe that's why many projects fail — common sense is just not applied. But it isn't just a lack of common sense that creates problems and, in some cases, causes failure; it's a lack of the necessary combination of learned skills, common sense and natural leadership ability. Project success depends on common sense project leadership.

Effective project management requires a unique skill set. The project manager must be competent in a variety of skills, such as project planning, estimating, use of software, scope management and resource leveling, to name a few. But to be truly effective, the project manager must also possess a significant number of soft skills, such as creativity, problem solving, verbal communication, conflict management, negotiating, influencing and team building. Additionally, the project manager must have business acumen and become familiar with budgeting, business case development, strategic thinking and tactical planning. Each of these skills and numerous others, are essential for the project manager to achieve success.

These skills can be found in most competency models designed to assess a project manager's overall ability and target areas where additional training, education and professional development are required. What isn't included in these competency models and other forms of assessment is a category called common sense.because in part, this can't be measured with a formal metric). Common sense is associated with sound judgment, and it's something that we learn over time. Common sense is also embedded in what most people define as leadership. Leadership also includes intuition, a sense of confidence, creativity and improvisation. Yes, we need the hard skills of project management but soft skills and sensible leadership are what really make a difference. Common sense may not be measurable but most of us will know when it isn't present.

A good source of common sense thinking and examples of effective leadership is *Fast Company* magazine. If I need an idea, something to jolt my thinking or just a different view of how to get things done, I turn to *Fast Company*. There is always an abundance of creative thinking and innovative ways to grow a business or turn around a problem area. Leadership techniques are embedded in just about every article. The magazine is not about project management; it's more about making sense of business and sharing the ideas of people who have "been there" and "done that", but with a burst of imagination and forward-thinking leadership. It's common sense business done uncommonly well.

As an example, one *Fast Company* article called "Balance is Bunk" discusses work-life balance. Basically, it says forget it, you just can't achieve it—but then it goes on to provide some sensible ideas on how to have a life anyway. Often, project managers must choose between family and the project, and the project often wins. There is a quote in the article, offered by John Wood, founder of Room to Read: "I don't look at balance as an ideal. What I look at is, am I happy? If the answer is yes, then everything else is inconsequential."[2] This is an example of common sense leadership. If you think about what Wood said, it makes perfect sense.

The question project managers have to ask themselves in their leadership positions is, "Am I happy?" A "yes" means that a form of balance has somehow been achieved, things are going well and whatever is being done makes sense. A "no" means that there are issues to address and a more sensible approach or solution is required. Sometimes we need a coach or a mentor to help us sort things out and set things right.

I think common sense escapes all of us from time to time and we need a little mentoring to get back on track. Here are some sensible suggestions inspired by the article:

- Set goals. Define what is truly important and develop a plan to achieve those things.
- Look at the long haul. Priorities will change depending on circumstances. Establish an order based on what's important at work and in life.
- Conduct a value assessment. Focus on items that you believe will contribute to your personal value and benefit the organization. Apply the eighty-twenty rule: 20 percent of what you do accounts for 80 percent of your value.
- Review and revise. Evaluate what you are doing and revise as needed. Justify the things you do to—and for—yourself and your family. Priorities will change and adjustments will be necessary. Give yourself frequent "value tune-ups."

Common sense leadership is essential for long-term success. Without it, the stress can cause early burnout and, in turn, significant problems with stakeholder relationships. People look to project managers for guidance and for help in making sensible decisions. I think it's important for the project manager to fill in those sensibility gaps and provide solid leadership for the team. If you observe effective leaders in action, their approach is generally the same. They seek to establish control and order, obtain the facts, provide direction, ask for suggestions, make decisions, follow up and provide feedback and encouragement. They provide the sensible approach that the team expects from a leader.

Another source of information that I have found extremely useful and inspiring is Roger Fulton's *Common Sense Leadership: A Handbook for Success as a Leader*. It talks about what a leader does, who a leader is and how a leader leads. It's filled with quotes and thought-provoking suggestions. A quote in the book sums up the discussion about common sense: "Common sense is the knack of seeing things as they are and then doing things as they ought to be done."[3]

Fulton also adds his thoughts about common sense. He says that it could be innate, come from experience or come from intelligence and knowledge, but the fact is a true leader has it, period![4]

Take a good look at how you and your team manage projects. How often does someone say, "That doesn't make sense!" or "Can you make some sense out of this?" Chances are you've made a similar statement at one time or another. Common sense is perceived to be in short supply but it is among us and our peers and always within our grasp. In the excitement of an unexpected problem or during an anxious moment, common sense is sometimes set aside or just simply forgotten. Take a minute or two to gather your thoughts, tap into that leader inside who is just waiting for the opportunity to help you get the job done and approach the situation with discipline. Common sense is sure to emerge. Leadership and common sense always seem to work together.

Your Personal Leadership Action Register

As you develop your leadership skills, you will notice that your decisions become more sensible, effective and defined. You will find that your ability to assess situations improves and you will become a person who people come to for advice. The common sense leader often becomes a mentor and helps to establish a culture of strong, well-balanced decision makers.

Develop a plan for your own personal growth as a leader. Each chapter contains many references and sources of information. Use these references and any personal notes you have documented to assist you in designing a plan that will achieve your leadership goals.

Make a note of insights, key learning points, personal recommendations, areas for review, books to read, self-development plans and topics of interest you would like to research.

_____

_____

_____

_____

_____

_____

_____

_____

_____

_____

_____

_____

_____

_____

_____

_____

Personal Leadership Activities
Figure 24.1

Action Item	Target Date for Completion
Review decisions made recently. Assess how the decisions were made and if another approach may have been appropriate	
Schedule a meeting with peers or your team and review a process that has been in place for a while. Use the discussion to determine if a better, more sensible approach could be developed	

25 Connecting with Executives

"If you're not confused, you're not paying attention."
— Tom Peters

"The manager asks how and when; the leader asks what and why."
— Warren Bennis

Project managers meet for several reasons. They discuss lessons learned and opportunities for improvement, celebrate project successes and network to obtain best practices that can be taken back to their own projects or Project Management Offices (PMOs). One subject widely discussed by project managers that seems to raise blood pressure, create anxiety and in some cases, genuine concern about future employment, is the gap between project managers and executives regarding the definition of project management and its value to an organization.

At a PMI Syracuse Chapter Meeting I attended, the evening presentation topic and the subject of some lively (to say the least) discussion was, "After forty years, why are we still trying to justify the profession of project management?" This may not apply to all organizations that manage projects but there is definitely a disconnect between project managers and executives about the value of project management, the role of the project manager and exactly what benefits that project management provides. A participant at the meeting shared a rather interesting and yet somewhat surprising, quote that was once offered by his project executive sponsor. The quote is something you should remember, as it gets at the very core of the issue of project management value. The quote was simple, straightforward and directed to the project manager. The executive said, "This project is going along very well, so what do I need you for?"

At first you may laugh and think this was just a joke, some professional levity not to be taken seriously. Unfortunately, it was expressed in a serious manner and took the project manager by surprise. Any project manager would immediately think, "I'm the reason things are going so well, so how about a little credit for that?" A natural reaction but credit is not something we should expect to receive regularly from project sponsors and executives.

In Dr. Harold Kerzner's book *Project Management: A Systems Approach to Planning, Scheduling, and Controlling*, he provides us with an interesting quotation: "Project management is the art of creating the illusion that any outcome is the result of a series of predetermined, deliberate acts when, in fact, it was dumb luck."[1] Many project managers are faced with this belief. It certainly isn't true in all organizations but for many of the project managers I have met through the years, this is a reality.

The challenge, therefore, is for project managers to connect with their project executives and senior management in a way that clearly demonstrates the value and strategic importance of project management. In the PMI® *Leadership in Project Management Annual*–2005 Volume 1, there is an article by Carlye Adler titled "Talk Elevated." It stresses the importance of speaking to executives in terms they will understand. If we associate this need to "talk elevated" with the concept of connective leadership, then we have the necessary ingredients to bridge the project manager/executive gap and make some real progress in elevating the perception of project management value in an organization.

In his article, Adler provides some examples of "Project Management Speak" versus "Executive Speak":[2]

Project Manager	Executive
Gantt chart	Timeline
Resource	Need specifics (people, money, supplies)
Delay or slippage	Reveal the problem and provide the solution
Objectives	Be specific (cash flow, measurable gains, etc.)
WBS	List of tasks
Critical path	Priority tasks
PMBOK® Guide	Documented best practices

As you can see, project managers speak at project level but it also important to speak at the executive level. During a discussion about the challenges a project manager must deal with (especially with executives), a colleague once said to me, "Executives don't need all that *PMBOK* stuff!" That didn't mean the *PMBOK Guide* was unimportant. It simply meant that executives are not interested in detailed steps and processes. I think that's true. Project managers need the "*PMBOK* stuff," but they need to translate it into Executive Speak!

Connective leadership creates an awareness of leadership styles that is direct, relational and instrumental. Each style has its own characteristics.

- The direct style is associated with people who work at an individual level to get things done and focus on how they will make their own contributions to the project or the organization.

- The relational style indicates a willingness to work with others to achieve results.
- The instrumental style refers those who look beyond existing boundaries and make new connections, breaking down barriers and establishing a more collaborative environment.[3]

If we combine the skills of connective leadership with talking elevated, we may have a formula for achieving executive level appreciation for project management.

The next time you are scheduled to meet with your project executive or senior management, take some time and review what you plan to tell them. Is it in the language they are used to hearing? Get a second opinion from a mentor or other reliable source and make sure you are talking elevated and connecting with your audience.

One of your goals as a project manager is to meet the expectations of your sponsors and executives. This can be more easily accomplished if a strong and trusting relationship is established between the project manager and executive. If you think about the basic communications model (Sender-Encoder-Region of Experience-Decoder-Receiver), we can see a direct relationship with the "talk elevated" and connective leadership approach. Establish an overlap between the executive region of experience and the project manager region of experience. The greater the overlap that exists within these regions of experience, the more effective and productive the communication will be. The end result should be a greater appreciation for project management and the project manager and a set of very clear, mutually-agreed-upon expectations. When you achieve that you will certainly be well-connected.

Your Personal Leadership Action Register

Think about how often you connect with executives. Is it very often? If you are an executive, how often do you connect with your project teams? What is your style of leadership? Teams that are well-connected with their leaders generally perform better and feel a sense of importance and value. Check on your connections and make sure you have continuity.

Develop a plan for your own personal growth as a leader. Each chapter contains many references and sources of information. Use these references and any personal notes you have documented to assist you in designing a plan that will achieve your leadership goals.

Make a note of insights, key learning points, personal recommendations, areas for review, books to read, self-development plans and topics of interest you would like to research.

_____
_____
_____
_____
_____
_____
_____
_____
_____
_____
_____
_____
_____
_____
_____
_____
_____

Personal Leadership Activities
Figure 25.1

Action Item	Target Date for Completion
Assess your ability to connect and communicate with executive management. Identify areas for improvement. Consider writing ability, presentation skills, and knowledge of the business and its objectives	

26 Elongate Your Dendrites

> "You can never solve a problem on the level on which it was created."
> — Albert Einstein

> "Creativity is a type of learning process where the teacher and the pupil are located in the same individual."
> — Arthur Koestler

What are dendrites? Good question. They are the branchlike parts of nerve cells within the brain that convey information. Research has found that highly educated people, curious learners, inventors and creative people have significantly longer dendrites than people who do not routinely exercise their brains. By exercise, I mean by reading, conducting research or otherwise challenging the brain through logic games, such as sudoku or other brain teasers. As an example, Einstein's brain showed the same results when examined—longer dendrites. He studied the universe, gave us the theory of relativity and asked lots of why questions. We can conclude from the research conducted about the human brain that the more you think about how to manage a problem from different perspectives or the more time you spend learning, thinking of innovative ways to achieve objectives or just imagining new things, you are elongating your dendrites. What does this mean to you as a project leader? From my perspective, it means that you should position yourself to be in a continuous learning mode, always seeking more knowledge, better ways to complete tasks and improving how team members work together. It means thinking creatively and encouraging others to do so. So, keep stretching those dendrites!

As Gary Fellers says in his book, *Creativity for Leaders*, we should "practice intense observation."[1] This provides us with an opportunity to really see how things are and how things work. It allows us to contemplate and imagine how things could be. Look at the environment around us—in our case, at the project environment. We should not only consider the project plan, how well the work is being performed and where variances exist, but we should also observe our teams in action, noting where things are going well and where there is opportunity to improve. In addition, it's important to look beyond the project environment and observe all aspects of your business. Ultimately, the project you are working on will have an impact on the organizational strategic plan and/or the financial bottom line (If your project is not in some way connected to strategic objectives, you may want to take another look at why you are working on it.)

Intense observation generates ideas, causes us to analyze what we see around us, and makes us question how work is performed and how things are done. Most project managers agree that there is always opportunity for improvement. When a project is completed, many project managers schedule post-project reviews to answer questions like: What worked well? What did we accomplish? What best practices were developed and where can we make improvements for use on the next project? If a methodology works well, it's a good practice to analyze it and find ways to make it work even better. The key is to ask the right questions because sometimes the very questions we ask can limit our thinking. Try to think differently during a review. Consider other questions besides: What can we do better the next time? Try some what if questions or ask the team to develop some scenarios that could possibly be encountered. Encourage your team to imagine their way through potential problems. Give them the opportunity to think about situations that could occur, and allow for some silliness to make it interesting. Many times, what seems like a very illogical approach actually turns out to be the basis for brilliant ideas.

Leadership competency improves when we take the time to observe. As Yogi Berra once said, "You can observe a lot by watching." There is a lot of opportunity for watching when we are leading projects. How are the team members getting along? Have you noticed any arguments among team members? What factors indicate a high-performing team? Are you communicating effectively to the team? How do you know? What's the informal buzz or grapevine telling you about your project or leadership style? How does your customer perceive the progress of the project? Besides project variances, such as schedule delays and cost overruns, what else is going on?

Take the pulse of the project. This practice of observing leads to questions, which lead to more questions and new, fresh answers. Some of the questions will require a healthy dose of creativity to solve, and creativity is a key quality of effective leaders. Not every answer can be found in a manual or a library of best practices. Sometimes the answer comes from looking at things from a completely different perspective, which generally means through several pairs of eyes.

There is one issue that requires some attention: Many project managers don't exercise the creative side of the brain. They believe that the answers to all problems can be found in previously written best practices or through subject matter experts who will use logic and experience to solve problems. That may be an effective method to solve many problems but since every project is unique, we need unique ways of thinking to get us through some of the tough issues.

Here is a checklist to help you elongate your dendrites. For each of these items, use some creative thinking to develop a continuous learning process that will help you generate new ideas and encourage your team to look at situations from different perspectives. Stand-up comedians use a similar process to generate new material. They look at everyday objects and ask themselves "what if" or "what would this do if I…" Just look at the props used by the popular Las Vegas comedian Carrot Top. He's a nonstop generator of new ideas, all coming from simple everyday objects. He just tries to look at them differently. He lets go of the normal and the logical. Project managers should also learn to look at things from several perspectives. Most major breakthrough inventions came from people who looked at problems and opportunities from a point of view that was very different from what is considered the norm.

Dendrite Stretchers
1. **Leadership** — Identify your values, your purpose and your vision. Are they aligned with the vision and objectives of your organization or your project? What changes can you make? What is working well? How do you know you are an effective leader? Where are changes required? What can you do to become more effective?

2. **Flexible Thinking and Resiliency** — Evaluate your ability to deal with a crisis situation. What questions do you ask when a problem arises? Are they the right questions? What behavior do you display during problem solving sessions? How do you inspire your team to come up with the best possible solutions? Instead of asking: "What's wrong?" or "What doesn't work?" Try asking, "What is working?" or "What can we use?" Think about Gene Kranz, the flight director for Apollo 13. He kept focused, stayed cool, displayed emotion when necessary and encouraged his team to do what the non-creative thinker would believe to be impossible. In one instance during the recovery efforts, he said to his team: "You're telling me what doesn't work and what [the command module] won't do. Tell me what it can do! Tell me what we can use!"[2]

3. **Communications** — Make sure you are clear when you communicate. Your team should understand your intentions. How can you ensure that you are effectively communicating with your team? How often do you obtain feedback from your team? How can you create a trusting environment that will encourage open and honest communication and feedback?

4. **Motivation** — Project leaders are challenged to find ways to keep their teams motivated. How can you assess your team's level of motivation? Does everyone buy into the project objectives? How do you know? How can you determine each team member's level of commitment? What behaviors are you displaying that are motivating the team? How can you improve your motivating skills?

5. **Holistic Thinking** — Do you look at your project as a complete system? What about how the project fits into the bigger business picture? How do you ensure that the project team has considered alternatives and that the best choices have been made?

Each of the items on the list will give you an opportunity to think differently. I don't like to use the term "out of the box" because it is used so much but it does fit well here. Forget the logical for a while and let go. There are ideas just waiting for a chance to emerge.

Hopefully, when future scientists study project managers of the 21st century, they will see what scientists learned about Einstein such as longer dendrites than those found in other leaders and managers, evidence of creative thinking and a passion for learning. So keep stretching those dendrites, challenge yourself and your team to learn and improve more rapidly, and look for, as von Oech says, "the other right answer."[3]

Your Personal Leadership Action Register

Projects give every project manager an opportunity to exercise their brain power. Look for opportunities to learn new things. Find out how to generate more creative thinking among team members. Take time each day and do a little imagining.

Develop a plan for your own personal growth as a leader. Each chapter contains many references and sources of information. Use these references and any personal notes you have documented to assist you in designing a plan that will achieve your leadership goals.

Make a note of insights, key learning points, personal recommendations, areas for review, books to read, self-development plans and topics of interest you would like to research.

Personal Leadership Activities
Figure 26.1

Action Item	Target Date for Completion
Try a few mind bender-type puzzles or some brain teasers	
Solve some math problems without a computer	
Try solving a crossword puzzle	
Conduct a creative problem solving session	

27 Achieving Extraordinary Results: The Leadership Formula

> "If your actions inspire others to dream more, learn more, do more and become more, you are a leader."
>
> — John Quincy Adams

With the economy still sluggish, a large number of companies are keeping their belts tight, watching costs and looking to reduce headcount. The position of the project manager remains as challenging today as it was back in the great "dot bomb" period of 1999–2002. An advertisement I saw for Microsoft Windows Server summed it up pretty well:

> "Larger projects, higher goals, greater responsibility, fewer resources, tighter timelines, and shrinking budgets."

It's interesting that the problems we are experiencing now haven't changed much from those of a decade ago. If you think about it, there isn't much more we can add to that list. I think most project managers can say: "Been there, done that," or more likely, "still there, still doing that." Technology provides part of the solution to these common project management issues, but technology is not the only solution. There are still many people involved in projects (estimates indicate that between fifteen and twenty million people around the world are either project managers or working on capital projects) in some capacity, who are working hard to keep from becoming another downsizing statistic. The project manager, therefore, has several major issues to deal with. At the top of the list are management's expectations which are generally associated with:

- the bottom line (financial benefit)
- connection with strategic direction and objectives
- the client's expectations (which are most likely about performance)
- delivery of the product
- quality
- cost
- perceived value of products and services

In addition, the project manager must be prepared to deal with the project team members who are concerned about their future and want to make sure they are connected to someone who can provide them with stability, a sense of confidence and a feeling of security. It's a list of challenges for any project manager, regardless of his or her experience. So what can a project manager do to succeed in such an environment? There is no single answer or magic formula. Or is there? A formula is defined as: "A conventionalized statement intended to express some fundamental truth or principle" or "a prescribed or set form or method."[1] Maybe there is a Leadership Formula hidden within all of the known characteristics required to be a leader. There is certainly no shortage of books and articles about leadership. You can find books about leadership in any major bookstore and a Google search about leadership will bring up more than 421 million results. Authors seem to be able to provide an endless supply of leadership success tools, techniques, principles, action items, self-development programs, suggestions, catchphrases and methods to help you motivate people.

If we dig through all of the available material, we may actually find what we are all looking for. Think of it as a form of treasure hunting. In this case, we are seeking the ultimate formula for truly effective leadership. It is kind of like seeking the Leadership Holy Grail. A friend once said to me: "There we were, working day and night,

night and day for ages until we ran into the obvious!" Sometimes what we are looking for is so close, so logical and so easy to reach that we just don't see it, or maybe we walk right past it. When it comes to leadership, each person must understand that, like projects, we as leaders are all unique. What works for one person may not work at all for someone else. It's also important for people who are in leadership positions, as well as those seeking leadership positions, to take time to assess themselves regarding leadership and then have someone else objectively assess their abilities.

A Leadership Formula? Yes! I think we can each create our own special blend with a little research, some reading, a little coaching and mentoring, and a very large dash of commitment. An article from *Fast Company* magazine, "How to Lead Now," provides many insights that can assist leaders in dealing with issues and focuses on how to obtain extraordinary performance when you can't pay top dollar for it. The answer is to treat people well. Show them you care, and be creative in how you influence them to perform the work at hand. Give them a voice in the decision process, show a little trust, and as it says in the article, make sure you find a way to feed them![2] The project leader did not have a budget of overtime but needed the team to be on the job for ten straight weeks of cutovers (a change from one technology to another or a change from one location to another, where organizational operations must be very well coordinated). The leader arranged for the team to organize theme dinners every Friday evening before the cutover began. This approach was a huge success and brought a sense of loyalty, fun and commitment to the project. Pretty creative, wouldn't you say?

As stated previously, there is an enormous amount of information available about leadership. I was particularly struck by a statement made by McDonald's founder Ray Kroc: "Happiness is a by-product of achievement." If an employee has pride in what he or she has done and the work is recognized, that employee will become a part of a winning team. Pride seems to be a key part of success, and leaders must find ways to cultivate pride. In fact, there is a book called *Why Pride Matters More Than Money*, by Jon R. Katzenbach. According to Katzenbach, the best leaders motivate along several themes.[3] It is more important to be proud of what you are doing than to simply focus on a goal. Goals are important but the journey to achieve a goal should be filled with rich experiences. To bring it all together, the leadership formula consists of:

- one part imagination
- one part innovation
- one part education
- one part mentoring
- one part self-confidence
- one part pride
- one part knowing your people and their needs
- a large portion of commitment
- some emotion
- a healthy amount of instilled pride (the pride you generate within the project team)

Mix in small portions to start so you are not overcome by any side effects or the potency of the formula. Brew larger portions as you adjust and share with associates. This is one formula that you want to become habit-forming.

Your Personal Leadership Action Register

Every leader develops a style and a set of principles. If you were to create a leadership formula, what ingredients would you use? Think about outstanding leaders who you have worked with or have read about and admired. How did they become great leaders?

Develop a plan for your own personal growth as a leader. Each chapter contains many references and sources of information. Use these references and any personal notes you have documented to assist you in designing a plan that will achieve your leadership goals.

Make a note of insights, key learning points, personal recommendations, areas for review, books to read, self-development plans and topics of interest you would like to research.

Personal Leadership Activities
Figure 27.1

Action Item	Target Date for Completion
Discuss the qualities and characteristics of a strong leader with your team. Find out how they define a leader	
Assess your leadership capabilities. Identify strengths and make note of your improvement areas	

28 WHERE HAVE ALL THE LEADERS GONE?

"Leaders must be close enough to relate to others, but far enough ahead to motivate them."
— JOHN C. MAXWELL

Lee Iacocca is a name familiar to many business leaders. He was CEO for Chrysler Corporation and the project manager for the renovation of Ellis Island, among other notable accomplishments. His experience and wisdom in the executive management community is well respected and sought after. Iacocca wrote the best-selling book, *Where Have All the Leaders Gone?* I was intrigued by the title and also interested in learning if he had the answer to that question. Some recent studies have shown that a large percentage of the U.S. population believe that a serious leadership crisis exists. A look at our recent history of corporate greed, ousted executives and disgraced political leaders provides plenty of evidence to support these studies.

Leadership is an integral part of project management. Anyone who steps up to the challenges of managing a project is also stepping into a leadership position. Iacocca's book is more directed toward the leadership issues associated with how the U.S. is managed, and the shortcomings of our elected officials, but it provides some excellent advice and insight for project managers, program managers and project executives. I personally think that every voting American should read the book. Iacocca provides some sorely needed straight talk about the issues we are facing as a nation and gives us quite a bit to think about, but the book also emphasizes some leadership factors that should be internalized by all project managers, regardless of project type or industry. I particularly like the suggestion to develop a leadership scorecard to assess how leaders are actually performing. This is a report card that clearly indicates just how well the leader is performing in various categories.

Iacocca developed a list of the "Nine Cs of Leadership," and suggests that we assess our leaders based on this list.[1] I think he captures the qualities that we expect to see in our leaders. I see a direct connection between this list of qualities and what we should expect from our project managers, sponsors and corporate executives. These items may not be new, but many have been forgotten or set aside, and should be reintroduced to leaders at every level, in every organization. In my career, I have often heard executives say: "We have to go back to the basics." Sometimes that is exactly the right thing to do. The "Nine Cs" provides the foundation that we need for leaders to grow and for new leaders to emerge.

"The Nine Cs of Leadership": The Project Management Perspective

1. **Curiosity** — Project managers should never be satisfied with the way things are. There are options to consider, new ways to achieve success and different methods and best practices in use by other organizations and industries. Stay curious and always look for ideas that will improve how your team accomplishes their assigned work.

2. **Creativity** — Today's changing project environment, rapid advances in technology and increased competition at the global level requires project managers to continually assess their project methodologies and how problems are solved. Lessons learned are definitely useful, but there is a need to encourage creativity and innovation within the project team and at the organizational level. Ask the "what if" questions and create scenarios and situations that require new ideas. Define project success in greater terms than on time, within budget and according to

specifications. Stir up the imagination of your team.

3. **Communication** — Communication is an essential skill for project managers but can be very complex and difficult to master. The true project leader excels at communication and is continually testing his or her effectiveness. Become an excellent listener, a source of information and encourage your team members to develop their skills. Take the time to understand the needs of the project stakeholders and learn more about their views and capabilities.

4. **Character** — The effective project manager has established a reputation of integrity and reliability. People respect and are influenced by leaders with character. True leaders know the difference between right and wrong, and how to use power in a positive way to achieve success.

5. **Courage** — The ability to make decisions. The ability to take a stand and take risks. The ability to accept the results of a decision. The ability to make a decision that may be unpopular but necessary. Project managers should have the ability to stand up for and protect their teams and willingly take on major challenges.

6. **Conviction** — Effective leaders have a visible passion for their work and for what they believe in. Leaders can develop that passion in their teams and create a loyal, high-performing team that is willing to step up to the daily challenges of the project environment and find solutions.

7. **Charisma** — The ability to inspire people and create a willingness to follow. This is not the charisma of the smooth talker or flashy dresser. This is the quality that causes people to take notice, to listen and want to contribute to the goals and objectives of the project or the organization.

8. **Competence** — Leaders understand the environment and its issues and have the ability to solve problems. This goes beyond technical knowledge and high IQ. It is the ability to assess situations, understand complex problems and develop effective and appropriate courses of action. It is the ability to generate confidence in the project team.

9. **Common Sense** — Project management has long been viewed as organized common sense. The project manager must apply a common sense approach to leading his or her team by knowing how things work, why things must be coordinated, who should be involved and who should contribute to decision making, as well as the consequences of a decision. Common sense means obtaining the right people and providing the right training and support that will inspire the team to succeed.

This list is a good test for leaders. Without these qualities, the leader cannot truly succeed and cannot build the trust, faith and commitment needed within an organization to achieve its objectives and continue to grow. Review the list and rate yourself. Develop a plan of action to address the areas that need attention, but also plan to continue to develop your strengths. When someone asks the question: "Where have all the leaders gone?" Let us make sure they are not directing that question to the project management community.

Your Personal Leadership Action Register

Consider your own organization. Should you be asking the question: "Where have all the leaders gone?" Make it a point to learn about leadership. Observe leaders in action. Look for opportunities to change the way the organization is managed and led. Focus on improvement and value-adding change.

Develop a plan for your own personal growth as a leader. Each chapter contains many references and sources of information. Use these references and any personal notes you have documented to assist you in designing a plan that will achieve your leadership goals.

Make a note of insights, key learning points, personal recommendations, areas for review, books to read, self-development plans and topics of interest you would like to research.

_____
_____
_____
_____
_____
_____
_____
_____
_____
_____
_____
_____
_____
_____
_____
_____
_____
_____

Personal Leadership Activities
Figure 28.1

Action Item	Target Date for Completion
Organize a leadership learning session. Discuss effective leadership techniques	
Observe your organization's leaders. What examples are they offering to aspiring leaders?	

29 THE LEADER AND CONFLICT MANAGEMENT

"Don't find fault, find a remedy."
— HENRY FORD

I recently read an article about conflict management that included the following quote: "Managing conflict is like riding a bicycle—all you need is balance and practice, practice, practice."[1] The article, called "Managing Conflict" by Angela Jackson, further mentioned that many people don't actually receive any type of formal training or instruction in managing conflict. They deal with conflict using the behaviors and approaches similar to that of their role models (parents, teachers, friends and other people of influence). Some role models choose to deal with conflict through force and power, while others may approach conflict in a cool and relaxed frame of mind. The results achieved using the techniques of the role model will generally be similar to the results the role model had achieved. These results may not provide the intended outcome.

Conflict certainly requires balance and each conflict we encounter provides us with a chance to learn. Returning to the bicycle analogy, it takes a fair amount of effort to achieve that balance. Some may choose a progressive approach, using training wheels, then a helping hand and eventually some solo efforts that are short in duration. Over time, confidence builds and longer and more challenging excursions are attempted. Others take the direct approach and ignore the need for safety and precautions. Generally, there will be a number of scraped elbows and knees when using this approach. Eventually balance is achieved, but there will always be a memory of mixed pain and pleasure upon achievement of balance. Later on, our method of teaching someone else to ride a bicycle could mean a repeat of that painful approach.

We all experience conflict in our business and personal lives. Conflict develops from many sources: differences of opinion, resource shortages, culture, religious beliefs, money or lack of it, values, ethics, prejudice and poor communication, to give a few examples. The leader or aspiring leader realizes that managing conflict is a necessary skill that must be developed and maintained. It is also something we can continuously learn from. Leaders become aware of their behaviors and understand that emotions, knee-jerk reactions and other spontaneous responses must be controlled. Most people have probably been through a conflict situation in which they walked away thinking, "That could have gone better."

I frequently mention a quote by Steven Covey when discussing communications and conflict management: "Seek first to understand and then to be understood."[2] If practiced, this statement can have a profound impact on the resolution of a conflict. Another favorite quote of mine (from my days back at AT&T in the operations environment, where conflict seemed to be the norm) is a statement made by a fellow supervisor who was witnessing a fairly intense argument: "No good advice was ever given at the top of one's lungs." I believe that's true and most of you who have had a conflict experience where shouting was involved will agree. To manage conflict effectively, we must first realize that our own behavior may be part of the issue. How we approach problems, and how we interact with people are key factors in conflict management. Here are some things to consider when you feel that a conflict may be developing:

1. Are you fully aware of what the conflict or potential conflict is about?

2. Do you have all of the facts available? Avoid opinions and hearsay.

3. Can you identify and explain the root causes of the conflict? Try to determine the source.

4. Avoid jumping to solutions. There are probably several options to consider. The first idea may not be the best and could be based on a gut-reaction.

5. What is your emotional state? If you are angry or upset, it is best to wait and regain your composure, balance and objectivity.

6. Is the person you are dealing with a friend, family or work associate? Your behavior will be a significant factor here and could result in some very unfortunate results if not carefully managed.

7. Consider the political ramifications of your approach. A very wise person once offered some advice when my project team was about to make a decision. He asked a straightforward, important question: "Are you fully aware of the implications of that decision?" This was his way of telling us that we really didn't think through the entire problem. Use the experts that you have available whenever possible to obtain that other perspective. You may want to ask yourself the same question if you are about to engage in a conflict, make a statement or take a course of action that you could regret later.

8. Review your actions and recent behavior. Did you do something that may have caused the problem? What did you do, and why did it result in a problem?

9. Avoid the use of words and phrases that can escalate a conflict. Words like never, always and should or phrases like: "You're totally wrong!" or "What's your problem?" can result in much more serious situations. These are referred to as load words, and are hurtful and usually result in a negative reaction.

10. What is the cost of being right? Sometimes it may be best not to pursue an issue. This is a real challenge, but it may be necessary to let it go. Is being right worth the loss of a friendship or other type of relationship?

11. Taking responsibility for solving a problem, regardless of who caused it, is better than seeking someone to blame.

12. Assess your listening skills. Make an effort to become an excellent listener. This means ignoring distractions and focusing on the views of other people involved. Demonstrating that you are listening is an effective way to reduce tension. Use phrases like: "Yes, I see your point" or "I was not aware of that."

13. Be prepared to stop the discussion if emotions become elevated. Plan to take a break to ensure that calmness is maintained or restored.

14. Discuss the situation with a trusted friend or mentor. An unbiased opinion can help you to see the other person's point of view more clearly.

15. Consider the problem and determine if the issue is actually something that is worth your time and effort. Sometimes we become involved in conflicts over things that in the larger scheme of things are quite trivial.

16. Stay focused on the problem. Avoid using other people and other issues to make a point. Many people tend to bring up the past or use unrelated stories to strengthen their position. Focus on the facts around the issue at hand. Defending a position usually results in an opposing position and progress can come to a grinding halt.

DEVELOPING AND USING PEACE PHRASES

Try thinking of peace phrases that can help you focus on the problem instead of the individual involved. Some examples of peace phrases are:

- "It's not you against me—it's you and me against the problem!"
- "We may not agree on everything, but let's try to find a way to at least respect each other's point of view."
- "We may not have a lot in common, but I'm thankful for your efforts to help meet the customer's needs. Your idea was quite useful."

"I" Statements

Use "I" Statements to describe a situation that will help the other person understand your point of view. "I" statements are familiar to many people who facilitate conflict situations. An "I" statement is a way to analyze and reframe a situation. A common framework for an "I" statement is I feel _____ when _____ because _____.

I feel _____ (put a name on the emotion and claim it)

Example: sad, betrayed, disrespected. It is a good idea to develop a feelings vocabulary to help you to express yourself clearly and effectively. A sample feelings vocabulary is sad, angry, frustrated, ashamed, surprised, shocked, hurt and disappointed.

When _____ (formulate a nonjudgmental description of the behavior)...

Example: You use my things without asking and don't return them.

Because _____ (describe the tangible effects of the behavior)...

Example: It prevents me from accomplishing something I committed to doing. It causes me to change my plans considerably and results in a delay.

Leaders know that there are many techniques for managing conflicts. Maintaining a balanced approach where both sides are considered, defining the problem clearly before taking action and focusing on the desired outcome will create an environment where conflicts can be resolved effectively.

Managing conflict is not easy. It takes effort, commitment and the ability to look past personal opinions and needs. Focusing on the actual problem and not on the other person will generally assist in resolving the issue. Seek advice from people who specialize in managing conflict and keep an open mind. In the project environment, the goal is not to win a conflict but to find a win-win solution.

Your Personal Leadership Action Register

Conflict is part of a project leader's everyday life. Preparing to manage conflict effectively will lead to greater leadership responsibilities and the admiration of peers, team members and executive managers. Conflict resolution skills should be found in every leader's toolkit.

Develop a plan for your own personal growth as a leader. Each chapter contains many references and sources of information. Use these references and any personal notes you have documented to assist you in designing a plan that will achieve your leadership goals.

Make a note of insights, key learning points, personal recommendations, areas for review, books to read, self-development plans and topics of interest you would like to research.

_____
_____
_____
_____
_____
_____
_____
_____
_____
_____
_____
_____
_____
_____
_____
_____

Personal Leadership Activities
Figure 29.1

Action Item	Target Date for Completion
Assess your personal conflict management style. Research available tools and determine if you need a conflict management tune-up	

30. The Art of Managing Expectations

> "A master can tell you what he expects of you. A teacher, though, awakens your own expectations."
>
> — Patricia Neal

Generally, discussions about leadership focus on the familiar characteristics of a leader and the external manifestations displayed by leaders, such as vision, ability to motivate, charisma, ability to communicate and so on. The question that is more difficult to answer is: What is leadership? To answer this question requires some thought about the people we believe to be true leaders. We need to ask ourselves: Why do I see this person as a leader? What did this leader accomplish? Having great communication skills, looking good for the cameras, knowing how to deliver a great speech and being charming and witty might be associated with many leaders, but these characteristics do not, in any way, reflect the actual capabilities of a person in terms of their ability to lead an organization or a team and accomplish great things. Leadership is much more than personality. Leadership is about creating change, taking risks, setting an example, leading the way and having the courage to keep trying when previous attempts did not work. Leadership is about filling people with a sense of confidence during difficult times, taking the edge off in times of stress and providing people with a sense of purpose and a belief that they can reach their goals.

Leadership begins with the development of a set of clear expectations. Unfortunately, in many cases, expectations are set in a very informal and sometimes hostile manner. When a new leader is assigned to a position or is brought on board, there is generally some type of dialog among employee and managerial levels about the incoming leader and what to expect. Many times these discussions are based on first impression and hearsay information. Assumptions are formed and plans for dealing with the new leader are often created well before the new leader's position actually becomes official. These assumptions and misguided observations may lead to communication barriers, stereotyping and an uncomfortable environment that could cause some serious issues in the areas of morale, respect and productivity. The newly assigned leader, upon some observation of the organization he or she is joining, may begin to set some expectations regarding organizational or specific individual performance without conducting any formal or informal discussions with other leaders or employees. This lack of dialogue about expectations can lead to a serious breakdown in many performance areas. Truly effective leaders understand that intentionally setting expectations is one of the key factors associated with organizational success. This means that the leader schedules a specific session to discuss issues, concerns, visions, ideas and other information that will help to establish a foundation for setting expectations. Ultimately, the expectations between an individual, a team or representatives from another business entity are established. It is important to understand that expectations are different from goals and objectives. Expectations are focused on how goals and objectives will be achieved.

Goals relate to vision, aspirations and a desired state. Everyone has or should have personal goals, such as becoming independently wealthy, achieving a dream job assignment, starting a business, writing a book or making a difference in a community. Organizations also have goals, like becoming the consumer's number one choice for products and services.

Objectives are the stepping stones to achieving goals and every organization ensures that they are set, reviewed, measured and reset when necessary.

Most project managers are familiar with **SMART** objectives:

S	=	**S**pecific	Clearly stated, detailed and focused.
M	=	**M**easurable	Can be tracked and measured in quantity, numerical data or comparative analysis.
A	=	**A**chievable	Feasible, actionable and can be accomplished by the assigned individual or team.
R	=	**R**ealistic	Meaningful and not beyond the capabilities of the individual or team and will produce a useful or value-adding result.
T	=	**T**ime-based	Will be accomplished within a reasonable timeframe and by an agreed-upon date.

Objectives answer the who, what, when, where, why and how. These questions establish direction for a team and are the foundation for any plan. We need objectives to make sure employees and teams are clear about direction and are on the same page about what must be accomplished.

Expectations are associated with objectives, but there are several differences. Expectations are more like agreements between people about how to proceed with an assignment, how reviews will be conducted during the execution of an assignment, how communication and changes will be managed and the level of quality, timeliness and reliability. As an example, a leader or manager may set the following expectation: "During this assignment I expect you to contact me immediately following a report of any safety violation." Or, "I expect you to keep me informed of major changes the customer may request."

Expectations are set in many ways. They can be communicated and established by what is said or not said, what someone else may have said or an action or inaction. It is important to ask the following questions to better understand a developing situation in which some type of action was taken or not taken: What made the person act in this manner? Why would the person approach the situation this way? How was this expectation set? Who set it? When was it set? What can you do about it? These are good questions but they are also reactive, so it may be more effective to ask the

following questions first:
- What am I expecting from the team or the individual?
- What do I know about the team or the individual?
- What is important to me regarding the assigned work or project? How important is timeliness? How important is format? How important are quality and ascetics?
- How well does the assigned individual know the process?
- How familiar is the individual with organizational policies?
- What is expected of me?
- How can I make sure that my expectations are clearly stated and understood?
- What is required to develop and deliver a clear expectation?
- What does the individual need to ensure a successful assignment?

The next time you have a conversation with a colleague about an unsatisfied client, manager or other business associate, you will probably hear someone make the following observation: "You didn't manage their expectations." Think about that statement. There is quite a bit of truth in those five words. If we use a familiar technique known as root cause analysis, it is possible to understand that many problems are created due to a lack of clearly defined and explained expectations. A simple form of root cause analysis requires a clearly stated and specific problem statement. Developing and articulating a clear and specific problem statement requires a little practice but it is essential for the process to work effectively. Defining a few basic categories to work with facilitate the process. The most common categories are:
- people
- equipment and machines
- methods
- materials

Think about a situation in which your expectations were not fully met. Then ask yourself how you know that the expectations were not met. What conditions were not satisfied? How do you know they were not satisfied? The problem may be that that you never actually explained your expectations. After some initial analysis you can probably generate a problem statement. Create a problem statement that specifically states which expectation was not met. For example: Performance has not reached the desired level. Then ask: What performance is in question? The question may relate to timeliness, a specific skill, absenteeism, following office policies, completing assignments, productivity or knowledge and comprehension, to name a few. Use this information to clarify the problem statement and ensure that you and others involved fully understand the problem.

Using the people category to begin the analysis, brainstorm some reasons why the problem could exist.

Example:
Problem statement: The employee does not fully complete assignments and all assignments require revisions by the manager.

ROOT CAUSE ANALYSIS CATEGORY: PEOPLE

Root causes: insufficient skills, unclear instructions, work overload, unwillingness to complete assignments, poor attitude, unable to learn.

From this information it is easy to determine that clearly defined expectations may be the real problem. There certainly may be other factors involved, but before drastic performance-improving measures and disciplinary actions are taken, it is a good idea to evaluate how effectively expectations were communicated in the first place. Many managers become involved in time-consuming negotiations and legal issues with employees who were disciplined or dismissed for performance reasons, when the real reason for the performance issue is directly connected to expectations that were not provided clearly and efficiently or managed on a regular basis. Think of setting clear expectations as a form of prevention against some major human resource problems.

Equipment, methods and materials may also contribute to the problem. Therefore, it is important to look at the whole picture before developing solutions and plans for action.

The good news is that the analysis of one particular problem can result in a solution that will prevent new problems from developing. A process for defining, communicating and managing expectations can result in higher levels of performance, improved morale and reduce the unpleasantness that often accompanies a performance appraisal.

It is the leader's role to create a vision, set direction and inspire followers. It is also the responsibility of the leader to establish a work environment where people know what is expected of them and that they will be treated fairly and with respect. Expectations involve both sides and require serious effort to develop, communicate and follow through to the end. The results of well-communicated and well-managed expectations benefit everyone. They can make a significant difference in the overall performance of an organization and have a very positive impact on organizational culture.

Your Personal Leadership Action Register

Consider the relationships you have with your team members and managers. Have you defined your expectations? Are you clear about what is expected of you? Is your team clear about what you expect from them?

Develop a plan for your own personal growth as a leader. Each chapter contains many references and sources of information. Use these references and any personal notes you have documented to assist you in designing a plan that will achieve your leadership goals.

Make a note of insights, key learning points, personal recommendations, areas for review, books to read, self-development plans and topics of interest you would like to research.

Personal Leadership Activities
Figure 30.1

Action Item	Target Date for Completion
Review expectations with my team and my immediate supervisor/manager	
Observe the team or an individual. Assess their performance and compare with previously established expectations	

31 Creating the Energy to Lead

"Leadership is the art of getting someone to do something you want done because he wants to do it."

— Dwight D. Eisenhower

True leaders seem to have an endless supply of energy. They accomplish great things, keep their followers engaged and loyal, and somehow always appear to be ready for the next challenge. They are calm during a crisis, decisive, confident and always have a word of appreciation for their team members.

Where does this energy come from? What fuels the drive of a leader? Your answer depends on how you define the word leader. Let's focus on the positive leader. The positive leader understands that the main ingredient in achieving a successful outcome to a challenge or an objective is the person who performs the task. They expect support, direction, protection from interference and meddling and appreciation for their work. The positive leader realizes that he or she must create an environment that provides a sense of support and a feeling that the work being performed is actually adding value. This is a tall order.

So how does a leader generate the energy required to lead? Part of the answer can be found in the following five steps:

1. Develop personal goals that are clearly defined and written. An important step in generating personal energy is to clearly define a set of personal goals. These goals should be realistic, non-competing (one goal does not undermine another goal) and should

be about things you really want. Create goals for your family and personal life, your professional career and your health. Simply having a set of goals will create an urge to move forward and achieve them. To help with this process, just imagine for a minute that you have reached one of the goals you've set. You can feel the energy within you beginning to build. That energy comes from a feeling of anticipated achievement.

2. Ensure that the work you do is interesting. People with just a touch of creativity and innovation can make even the most mundane work seem interesting. Attitude is a key factor. The leader sees opportunity in all work. The leader also knows that the work performed and the results achieved are a reflection of the leader's true value. If work is to be performed, the work should be necessary and should contribute to the higher goals of the organization. The leader seeks work that will result in an increase in personal value and performs work that will interest others.

3. Ensure that the work you do is challenging. The leader seeks and accepts challenging assignments that other people might shy away from. A good challenge sparks the imagination and causes the mind to come alive with ideas. A challenge asks to be overcome and ignites the energy cells within the leader.

4. Perform work that will be appreciated. At any level of an organization there is work that must be performed. Regardless of the type of organization, there is always someone who the leader reports to, and all leaders are expected make a contribution. The positive leader performs his or her assignments with a high degree of enthusiasm and professionalism, focuses on quality and has an understanding that the work has been assigned for a reason and is worth performing well. Partially completed work, poor quality and late

completion of assignments are not associated with the characteristics of a successful leader.

5. Identify work that will add value. The positive leader focuses on work that will add value to the organization and enhance his or her personal value. The work may be associated with improving the financial condition of the organization or the reputation of the brand. The work may be designed to increase the loyalty of the employees or create a greater bond with customers. In any case, the work that leaders perform is not accidental. There is real purpose involved.

There are leaders at every level of an organization and anyone who identifies and performs value adding work is a leader. The energy that drives the leader also creates the environment that will motivate the team. A team that observes a leader who shows genuine interest in his or her work, and the work of the team will create a sense of accountability within the team. Effective leaders show clear appreciation for the work performed by the team, and will challenge the team to reach beyond their perceived limitations, creating a positively-charged organization.

Your Personal Leadership Action Register

The stories, ideas and suggestions in the previous chapters will assist you in enhancing your leadership skills. These suggestions may create a spark in your imagination or inspire you to make a change that can completely revitalize your leadership journey. Take the time to make notes about what you could do to become a more effective leader or mentor. There is always something that you can do differently or better. Take advantage of your creativity and imagination. Find new ways to make a difference.

Personal Leadership Activities
Figure 31.1

Action Item	Target Date for Completion
I can make a difference right now by…	

32 Lessons Learned From the Last Lecture

> "Life is not about the mistakes you've made, but the lessons you've learned."
> — Unknown

Several years ago at a PMI® Seminar/Symposium (before they were renamed PMI® Global Congresses), I attended a keynote presentation offered by Bob Ross, author of *Laugh, Lead and Profit: Building Productive Workplaces with Humor*.[1] It was a particularly enjoyable presentation, filled with good advice and of course, tasteful humor. As with many presentations we attend, we sometimes pick up a gem or two of wisdom that stays with us and is never very far from our conscious, daily thoughts. The gem I picked up back then (which I mentioned in a previous chapter) was actually a question that Ross asked at the conclusion of the speech:

> "When you leave this earth, will you leave a vacancy or a void?"

Anyone can fill a vacancy but a void is something that people really notice. In the project management community, there are so many people who have contributed to furthering the value of project management. Kerzner, Wideman, Lewis, Cleland, Meredith, Mantell and Hillson are a few individuals who have provided knowledge, wisdom and insight for both the new and the seasoned project manager. These individuals have made many significant contributions to the project management environment and will leave a legacy of value.

There are many sources of information about project management, including the writings of well-known experts and the shared knowledge of professional organizations. Sometimes the knowledge and wisdom we obtain comes from sources outside of this familiar territory. We often look for advice and knowledge from subject matter experts and knowledge champions. They are most often part of the universe in which we live and work. Often, when we step outside of that universe we discover something new or maybe a different way of seeing things. This discovery is a kind of awakening, and one of my discoveries was *The Last Lecture*.

The Last Lecture, by Randy Pausch, is certainly not a book you would expect to find in the world of project management literature. While Pausch was a professor at Carnegie Mellon, he was diagnosed with pancreatic cancer and after many attempts at fighting the disease, he was given only a short time to live. While he was struggling with the disease and focusing on the needs of his family, he was given an opportunity to be the speaker in a series titled "The Last Lecture." There was clearly a certain irony in this opportunity. Pausch decided that it was important to fulfill his commitment to participate in the series, despite many other pressing needs, especially those associated with his family.

Pausch delivered a lecture that has been viewed by millions via the internet and there is no doubt that he left a void with his untimely departure. The book is based on his journey to The Last Lecture and captures far more than what he could say in that hour-long segment. The story that leads up to The Last Lecture is inspiring and compelling. There is no doubt that anyone who has read the book has experienced the emotion, passion and desire to make a difference expressed by Pausch. His goal was to care for his family and to leave a legacy about the joy of life and the importance of working toward fulfilling your dreams. His bond with his family is inspiring and his desire to help others - especially his students - is unmistakable.

I am not sure if he intended for his thoughts and wisdom to fit within the topic of leadership but his book is filled with lessons learned about life, and the importance of helping others find their way to success and fulfillment. His message is about giving others an opportunity to grow and to encourage creativity, innovation and imagination. Pausch was a Walt Disney Imagineer (a combination of "imagination" and "engineer," a term coined by Disney). His life was filled with dreams and he worked very hard to have them become a reality. His advice will assist aspiring leaders, as well as the most experienced and well-respected leaders. The best way to obtain the value and to experience Randy's wisdom and passion is to read the book and view The Last Lecture online. You will not only be touched by his thoughtfulness and his honesty, but you will be inspired to examine your own dreams and your current reality and develop a plan of your own to make a difference.

SOME LESSONS LEARNED

- **Find what makes you unique** — What defines you and your existence? There is something unique about everyone. Being a project manager doesn't make you unique and being a leader really doesn't either. You have to examine what you have accomplished throughout your life and what dreams you have fulfilled. Take the time to look back and look ahead. Focus on achieving your dreams. The stories about how you achieved each of your dreams are what make you unique.
- **The elephant in the room** — Sometimes there is something so obvious that it can take up a lot of space (specifically the attention of others), and yet it is not addressed. The lesson is to take care of that elephant in the room so you can focus on more important issues.
- **Be creative** — Let your imagination go. Let it work. Look at things differently. Have fun! Encourage others to be creative.
- **If you can find an opening, you can probably find a way to float through it** — If you have a goal - maybe just a dream - and you work at it with determination, you can create an opportunity to fulfill it.
- **Fundamentals** — Make it a point to get to know what others are doing. Teamwork, perseverance, sportsmanship,

the value of hard work and dealing with adversity are truly important.
- **Leadership** — Understand what it means. Learn it from others who seem to excel at it. Identify a role model and a mentor.
- **Think positive** — At Disney World, when a guest asks a staff member what time the park closes, they are told that it's open until eight p.m.—a positive response to the question. Randy Pausch, throughout his ordeal, managed to think positively about life. There were some trying times but his message was clear: You have to work with the cards you are dealt. He did his best to ensure that he lived his life with meaning, and that he valued every day he lived. He saw value in other people and mentored many of his students. He helped his students to help themselves and many of them became successful. He demonstrated his pride in the achievements of people he helped and acknowledged them for their successes.

The Last Lecture will make a profound impression. It is a book you will want to read again and again, or just skim through from time to time to refresh your memory of the many bits of knowledge and advice. Many times in the book, Pausch mentions the concept of a "head fake."[2] Through this concept, he is teaching you about something that seems very specific and obvious, but actually teaches you something that will remain with you for a lifetime, that you don't realize you are learning until well into the learning process. Perhaps one of Pausch's most important head fakes are the lessons learned about leadership embedded in his book. They don't jump out at first but as you read each chapter you realize that there is more going on than just a story. Randy Pausch created a void that can never be filled. He made a difference, and he was clearly a leader.

Your Personal Leadership Action Register

The Last Lecture encourages people to look closely at their own lives and to find ways to appreciate what is most important - finding personal fulfillment, helping others and believing in your own capabilities.

Develop a plan for your own personal growth as a leader. Each chapter contains many references and sources of information. Use these references and any personal notes you have documented to assist you in designing a plan that will achieve your leadership goals.

Make a note of insights, key learning points, personal recommendations, areas for review, books to read, self-development plans and topics of interest you would like to research.

Personal Leadership Activities
Figure 32.1

Action Item	Target Date for Completion
Revisit my dreams and plan to achieve them	
Become a mentor	

Final Thoughts

Leaders should always strive for a positively-charged organization. This type of organization has everyone seeking new ways to move the organization to the next level of performance. Each person within the company sees himself or herself as a partner in leadership, adapting as needed to changing demands and business environments while keeping an eye on the horizon.

Organizations that support a Positive Leadership approach create a balance between individual development and accomplishment and achievement of the organization's collective goals. There are difficult times to manage through and tough decisions to make, but positive leaders accept the responsibilities that come with the position and always look for the new opportunities sometimes masked by challenges.

The leadership journey can be expected to include a number of obstacles. The path will not always be easy. There will be unexpected changes along the way, and encounters with many new people who will offer different points of view. There will be some conflict, some critical decisions to make and mistakes to learn from.

Fortunately, it's not difficult to equip yourself for the journey. The resources available to the aspiring, as well as the experienced leader are abundant. An important factor is to remain in a learning mode. In addition, the desire to keep learning is important to demonstrate as well as respect for others, professionalism at all times and an understanding of the need to balance personal and professional life as well as the desire to succeed along with an inspiring personal vision and sustaining self-confidence — especially during the most difficult times.

Keep your focus on the positive side of leadership. The greatest leaders focus more on helping others to succeed and less on seeking the spotlight. Make sure that you show your appreciation for your team. That's Positive Leadership in project management. Enjoy your journey.

Notes

*Portions of this book originated from various articles written by Frank P. Saladis, PMP, for *allPM* (www.allpm.com). *allPM* is a free global resource for project managers around the world. All permissions and rights for this material have been granted by *allPM* and its parent company, International Institute for Learning, Inc. (www.iil.com).

An Introduction
1. Covey, Stephen R., Merrill, Roger A., and Merrill, Rebecca R. , *First Things First,* (UK, Simon & Schuster 1999) 77.

Chapter 1
1. Warner, Fara, "Keeping the Crisis in Chrysler," *Fast Company*, September 1, 2005, 1. http://www.fastcompany.com/magazine/98/chrysler.html?page=0%2C3.

2. Warner, Fara, "Keeping the Crisis in Chrysler," *Fast Company*. "Keep you back to the wall" is Frank Saladis' interpretation from one of the article's several suggestions for managing success.

3. Warner, Fara, "Keeping the Crisis in Chrysler," *Fast Company*. Frank Saladis' interpretation of article's emphasis on the customer.

4. Umlas, Judith W. *The Power of Acknowledgment*, New York: IIL Publishing, 2006. "The 7 Principles of Acknowledgment" are an excerpt from *The Power of Acknowledgment*©.

Chapter 2

1. Verma, Vijay, *Human Resource Skills for The Project Manager, Volume 2, Project Management, Institute*, (Pennsylvania, Project Management Institute 1996), 221.

2. Batten, J.D., *Tough Minded Leadership*, (New York, AMACOM, 1989), 35.

3. Verma, Vijay, *Human Resource Skills for The Project Manager, Volume 2, Project Management, Institute*, (PA, Project Management Institute 1996), 220.

4. *PMI Role Delineation Study*: The Project Management Institute, PMI conducts a role delineation study for the Project Management Professional PMP credential every five to seven years to ensure the credential reflects contemporary practice and evolves to meet current needs in the profession. (PA: The Project Management Institute, PMI, 1996). http://www.pmi.org/passport/dec10/passport_dec10_in-the-news.html.

5. SWOT Analysis (Strengths Weaknesses, Opportunities, and Threats) http://en.wikipedia.org/wiki/SWOT_analysis. Originally created as SOFT Analysis by Albert Humphrey, Stanford University. http://en.wikipedia.org/wiki/Albert_S_Humphrey.

Chapter 4

1. *Merriam-Webster OnLine*, s.v. "Savvy," accessed March, 15, 2012, http://www.merriam-webster.com/dictionary/savvy?-show=1&t=1334325883

2. *Merriam-Webster OnLine*, s.v. "Savvy," accessed March 15, 2012, http://www.merriam-webster.com/dictionary/savvy?-show=1&t=1334325883

3. Heerkens, Gary, *The Business Savvy Project Manager*, (New York: McGraw-Hill Companies Inc., 2006), 4.

4. Ibid.; 12.

5. Wysocki, Robert, and Lewis, James P., *The World Class Project Manager*, (MA: Perseus Publishing, 2001), 87-91.

6. Project Management Institute, "Organizational Process Assets," *PMBOK Guide®* 4th Edition, (PA: The Project Management Institute, PMI ®, 1996), 32. http://marketplace.pmi.org/Pages/ProductDetail.aspx?GMProduct=00101095501.

7. Heerkens, *The Business Savvy Project Manager*, 4.

8. *PMBOK Guide®* 4th Edition, 6.

9. *International Project Management Day Webinar* (hosted by New York, New York: International Institute for Learning, Inc., November 2005). Ron Kemp, Director, HP Project Management; COE & featured speaker for the IPMDay, November 2005.

Chapter 5

1. Kerzner, Harold Ph.D. and Saladis, Frank P., PMP., *Value Driven Project Management*. (The IIL-Wiley Series in Project Management) New York: International Institute for Learning, Inc.; IIL Publishing & New Jersey: Wiley, 2009.

2. Kerzner and Saladis, *Value Driven Project Management*, 2009.

3. Pinto, Jeffrey K., "The Elements of Project Success," in *The Field Guide to Project Management,* 2nd Edition, ed. David Cleland, (New Jersey: John Wiley & Sons, 2004), 24.

Chapter 6

1. *The Last Castle*. Directed by Rod Luri. (2001, Nashville, TN; Paramount Home Videos, 2004) DVD.

2. Giuliani, Rudolph W., *Leadership*, 1st Edition. New York: Hyperion, October 1, 2002.

3. Ibid.; 123

Chapter 7

1. Middleton, Drew, "The Soldiers General" The Soldiers General, *NY Times*, 1983.

2. Bradley, Omar N. and Blair, Clay, *A General's Life*, an Autobiography (New York: Simon & Schuster, February 1983), 752.

3. Brighton, Terry, *Patton, Montgomery, & Rommel - Masters of War* (New York: Three Rivers Press, Div. of Random House Inc., 2008).

Chapter 8

1. Kerzner, Harold Ph.D., *Project Management – A Systems Approach to Planning, Scheduling, and Controlling,* 10th Edition, (New Jersey: John Wiley & Sons, March 23, 2009), 181-182.

Chapter 9

1. Friedman, Thomas L., *The World is Flat: A Brief History of The Twenty-First Century* 1st Edition, (New York: Farrar, Straus and Giroux, 2005), 1-17.

2. Lee, Shelton, *Creating Teamwork*, Boulder, CO: Career Track Publications, 1986. Audiobook on Cassette.

3. Giuliani, Rudolph W., *Leadership*, 1st Edition (New York: Hyperion, 2002), 1-26.

Chapter 10

1. Goldsmith, Marshall, "Don't Just Check the Box," *Fast Company Magazine,* February, 2005. http://www.fastcompany.com/magazine/91/mgoldsmith.html.

CHAPTER 11

1. Saladis, Frank P., "Professional Services Project Management: Real Stories of Project Management," City: Cisco Systems 1999-2001. *study conducted by Frank P. Saladis for this paper and presentation; originally for Cisco and updated independently in 2005 and 2010.*

CHAPTER 12

1. Wess, Roberts, Ph.D. and Ross, Bill, "Authors Note," in *Make It So – Leadership Lessons from Star Trek, The Next Generation* (NYC: Pocket Books,1995), xi.

2. Wess, Roberts, Ph.D. and Ross, Bill, *Make It So: Lessons Learned – Leadership Lessons from Star Trek, The Next* Generation. NYC: Pocket Books,1995.

3. Saladis, Frank P., "Lead Like Everyone is Watching," in (former) *allPM Website*, New York: IIL Publishing, 2003.

4. Wess, Roberts, Ph.D. and Ross, Bill, "Authors Note," in *Make It So – Leadership Lessons from Star Trek, The Next Generation* (New York: Pocket Books,1995), xiii.

5. Horning, Jim, http://en.wikiquote.org/wiki/Jim_Horning who at-tributes to the original Mulla Nasrudin http://virtualbumperstickers.blogspot.com/2007/06/good-judgment-comes-from-experience.html.

CHAPTER 13

1. Carr, Kathleen, "A New World Order," *Continental Airlines Magazine*, March 2006.

Chapter 14

1. Ross, Bob, "Lead, Laugh and Profit," (Keynote Speaker, Project Management Institute - PMI ®, New Orleans, 1995). Bob Ross is author of *Lead Laugh and Profit,* San Diego CA: Arrowhead Publishing, 1989.

Chapter 15

1. Von Oech, Roger, *A Whack on the Side of the Head,* (New York, New York: Warner Books, 1983), Revised Edition (Stamford, CT: U.S. Games Systems, Inc. 1990), 4-6.

2. Ibid., 11.

3. Ibid., 6.

4. Ibid., 9.

Chapter 16

1. Knutson, Joan, "A Project Management Renaissance: The Future is Already Here," *PMNetwork,* July, 2003.

2. *Wikipedia*, "Louis Pasteur (December 27, 1822 – September 28, 1895), French microbiologist and chemist," http://en.wikiquote.org/wiki/Louis_Pasteur.

Chapter 17

1. *Retaining Your Best People*, Boston, MA: Harvard Business School Press, 2006.

2. Tom Peters, *The Pursuit of WOW! Every Person's Guide to Topsy-Turvy Times*, New York: Vintage Books, A Division of Random House Inc., 1994. Also see - Tom Peters, "The Wow Project," *Fast Company Magazine*, May 1999, Vol 24. http://www.fastcompany.com/magazine/24/wowproj.html.

CHAPTER 18

1. *Magnum Force*, directed by Ted Post (1973; Burbank, CA: Warner Home Video, 2001), DVD.

2. Peters, Tom, *The Pursuit of Wow! Every Person's Guide to Topsy-Turvy Times* (New York: Vintage Books, 1994), xi - xii.

CHAPTER 20

1. Lipman-Blumen, Jean, *Connective Leadership: Managing in a Changing World*, New York: Oxford University Press, 1996, Paperback edition, 2000.

2. Ibid., 113 -165.

3. Project Management Institute, "A Guide to the Project Management Body of Knowledge" *PMBOK® Guide,* 4th Edition, (Newton Square, PA: Project Management Institute ®, 2008), 13, 215, 229. www.pmi.org.

4. Kouzes, James M. and Posner, Barry Z., *The Leadership Challenge: How to Get Extraordinary Things Done in Organizations* (San Francisco: Jossey-Bass, 1995), 134 -137.

5. *Merriam-Webster OnLine,* s.v. "Kinetic," accessed April 29, 2012. http://www.merriam-webster.com/dictionary/+kinetic?-show=0&t=1334853351.

6. *Merriam-Webster OnLine,* s.v. "Energy," accessed April 29, 2012. http://www.merriam-webster.com/dictionary/%20energy.

7. *Merriam-Webster OnLine,* s.v. "Kinetic Energy," accessed April 29, 2012. http://www.merriam-webster.com/dictionary/kinetic+energy?show=0&t=1334852398.

Chapter 21

1. Study about non-verbal communication. This controlled Study was conducted in 1967 by Dr. Albert Mehrabian, a Professor of Psychology at UCLA.

2. Peters, Tom, *The Pursuit of Wow! Every Person's Guide to Topsy-Turvy Times.* New York: Vintage Books, 1994. The term **Wow!ers** is not in the book; it is an interpretation of what Tom Peters was professing.

3. Peters, Tom, *The Pursuit of Wow! Every Person's Guide to Topsy-Turvy Times* (New York: Vintage Books, 1994), 39.

Chapter 22

1. Project Management Institute, "A Guide to the Project Management Body of Knowledge" *PMBOK Guide,* Fourth Edition, (Newton Square, PA: Project Management Institute ®, 2008) 215, 229. www.pmi.org.

2. *Magnum Force,* directed by Ted Post (1973; Burbank, CA: Warner Home Video, 2001), DVD.

Chapter 23

1. von Oech, Roger, *A Whack on the Side of the Head: How to Unlock Your Mind for Innovation* (New York: Warner Books, 1988), 50-53.

2. Ibid., 50.

3. Ibid., 50.

Chapter 24

1. Covey, Stephen R., *The 7 Habits of Highly Effective People* (New York: Free Press, 2004), 7-8. This statement was articulated in his audio book and during his seminars.

2. Hammonds, Keith H., "Balance is Bunk!," *Fast Company*, December 19, 2007. http://www.fastcompany.com/magazine/87/balance-1.html.

3. Fulton, Roger, *Common Sense Leadership: A Handbook for Success as a Leader* (New York: Barnes & Noble Books, 2001), 94.

4. Ibid., 94.

Chapter 25

1. Kerzner, Harold Ph.D., *Project Management: A Systems Approach to Planning, Scheduling, and Controlling* (Hoboken: Wiley, 2009), 4.

2. Adler, Carlye, "Talk Elevated," *Leadership in Project Management Annual*–2005 Volume 1,

3. Lipman-Blumen, Jean, *Connective Leadership: Managing in a Changing World* (New York: Oxford University Press, 2000), 113-165.

Chapter 26

1. Fellers, Gary, *Creativity for Leaders* (Gretna: Pelican Publishing, 1995), 18.

2. Apollo 13 Directed by Ron Howard. (1995: Universal Pictures, CA; HD DVD, 2006).

3. von Oech, Roger, *A Whack on the Side of the Head: How to Unlock Your Mind for Innovation* (New York: Warner Books, 1988), 21.

Chapter 27

1. *Merriam-Webster OnLine*, s.v. "Formula," accessed May, 5, 2012. http://www.merriam-webster.com/dictionary/savvy?show=1&t=1334325883

2. Byrne, John A., "How to Lead Now," *Fast Company*, December 2007, www.fastcompany.com/magazine/73/leadnow.html

3. Katzenbach, Jon R., *Why Pride Matters More Than Money*, New York: Random House, 2003.

Chapter 28

1. Iacocca, Lee, *Where Have All the Leaders Gone?* (New York: Scribner, 2007), 3-14.

Chapter 29

1. Jackson, Angela, "Managing Conflict," *Presentation Pointers*, article id232. www.presentation-pointers.com.

2. Covey, Stephen R., *The 7 Habits of Highly Effective People*, (New York: Free Press, 2004), 235.

Chapter 32

1. Ross, Bob, *Keynote Address*, (New Orleans: PMI Annual Seminars and Symposiums, 1995, Keynote address). Also, Author of *Laugh, Lead and Profit*, (San Diego: Arrowhead Publishing, 1989).

2. Pausch, Randy, *The Last Lecture*, (New York: Hyperion Books, 2008), 35-39.

Index

A
acceptance criteria, 41, 90, 107, 108,
accomplishments, assessing, 53, 144
achievement of extraordinary results, leadership formula, 199-203
active listening, xviii
activity words, 157
Adams, John Quincy, 199
adaptive leadership, 127
Adler, Carl, 186-187
ambition, leadership and, 100
Apollo 13 mission, 194
Apollo 13 (movie), 139
Aslan Phenomenon, 174
"Away Teams", 98, 100

B
balance, xx-xvi
"Balance Is Bunk", 180
Batten, J. D., 10
behavioral considerations in project failures, xi
Bennis, Warren, 185
Berra, Yogi, 193
body language, 164
Bradley, Omar, 60
budgeting, 27-28, 179
business assessment, 27-28
business case justification, 28
business functions, 28
business process design, 28
The Business Savvy Project Manager, 26
business savvy, project managers and, 26, 29-30
    important skills for project managers, 27
    thinking like a CEO, 126
business skills, 26-28, 31, 32

C
Callaghan, James, 163
Carr, Kathleen, 105
Carrot Top, 193
Cashman, Kevin, xix
certainty words, 157
character, 21, 24, 105, 112, 207
charisma, iii, 113, 207, 219
check the box approach, 82-83
closure, project
    recognize, reward, and rest, 2
communications
    active listening, xviii
    basic model, 84, 188
    dendrite stretchers, 194
    effective, through feedback and follow-up, 164
    questions to ask to improve communications, 194, 212
    in definition of leadership, 91
    maintaining leadership role with, 91
    in Nine Cs of Leadership, 206
    nonverbal, 164
    in positive leadership, 153-154
    between project managers and executives, 92, 160
    using to retain key team members, 131
commitment to the project, 81, 112
commitments, keeping, 14, 39, 77
common sense, 179
Common Sense Leadership: A Handbook for Success as a Leader, 181

common sense project leadership, 179-182
complacency, 2, 118
company products and services, 28
competence, 208
competencies (key), of project managers, 90-91
competency and effectiveness, higher levels of, 27-46
completion of projects, major issues affecting, 89-90, 92
conflict management, 211-215
  considerations when conflict is developing, 212
  "I" statements, 215
  peace phrases, 214
connective leadership, 153-160
  communication between project managers and executives, 157
  connectic energy, defined, 159
  defined, 159
  instrumental leadership, 156-159
  interdependence in project environment, 155
  styles of leadership, xvi, 53 155
  summary of its goals and functions, 159
Connective Leadership: Managing in a Changing World, 155
consensus leadership, 51
continuing cycle of leadership, 75
conviction, 207
core application systems, 28
Cosby, Bill, 170
cost
  as part of triple constraint, 26
  and retention of key team members, 133
courage, 207
Covey, Stephen R., 1xv, 179, 212
creativity, 50

challenging rules and status quo, 157
elongating your dendrites, 191-195
in project team, importance of, 117-120
Creativity for Leaders, 192
cultural differences, 74
customer driven, 105
curiosity, 206
customer satisfaction
  defining success, 3, 5-6, 36
customer service, 28
customers
  customer-supplier model, 108
  as drivers of business decisions, 22
  project team members as, 105

D
decision making, 21, 112, 208
decisions, evaluating, 52
dendrites, elongating, 191-195
destructive roles, project team members, 66
direction
  sense of, xv, 84, 131
  setting, 123, 156-157
direct leadership, 148, 155, 187
Dirksen, Everett, 139
disruptive attendees of meetings, 21
discovery, 118
Disney, Walt, 193, 235
diversity
  in today's workforce, 73
  and working effectively together, 97
Dole, Elizabeth, 131
"Don't Just Check the Box", 82
dreams, achieving, 234-236

E
Eastwood, Clint, 142, 169

eonomic problems, current, 198
education and training, 125
    being in continuous learning mode, 191
effectiveness and competency, 12-15
ego, leadership and, 59, 60, 61, 99-101
Eisenhower, Dwight D., 117, 227
Einstein, Albert, 191
elephant in the room, 235
emotional commitment, 166
enabling/empowering others, 170
energy, 160
    creating energy to lead, 227-229
    leaders as source of, 169-170
engineers as project managers, x
enthusiasm, displaying, 141
    wow! leadership and projects, 164-165
executives, connecting with, 185-190
connective leadership, combining with talking elevated, 186
    project management speak vs. executive speak, 187
expectations
    managing, 219-226
    setting, 105

F

failure (personal), trying to please everyone, 170
failure of projects
    behavioral considerations in, x
    examining to find different approach, 176
Fast Company magazine, 1-3, 82
feedback, 11
    asking for and keeping open mind on, 134-135
    effective communication through, 82-85
    about leadership effectiveness, 141
    providing to retain key team members, 134
feeding project members, 201
Fellers, Gary, 192
Field Guide to Project Management, 2nd Edition, 38
financial investments, projects as, 26
financial savvy, 25
First Things First, xv
flexible thinking and resiliency, 194
The Flight of the Phoenix, 176
follow-up, effective communication through, 81-85
Ford, Henry, 89, 211
foundation values, 37
Friedman, Edwin H., 123
Friedman, Thomas L., 74
Fulton, Roger, 181-182
fundamentals, 235
future, preparing for, 123-127
    suggestions, 125-127

G

Galbraith, John Kenneth, 19
Gardner, John, 163
general managers, project managers and, 29-31
generation X and Y employees (millennials), motivation of, 133
Giuliani, Rudolph W., 51
goals, xv
    expectations versus, 221
    knowing when they can't be achieved, 159
    personal, developing, 227-228
Goldsmith, Marshall, 82
A Guide to the Project Management Body of Knowledge (PMBOK® Guide), 156. *See also* PMI

H

happiness
    balance and, 180

as by-product of achievement, 201
head fakes, 236
help, asking for, 170
Heerkens, Gary, vii, 25-26
Hesselbein, Frances, 105
holistic thinking, 195
"How to Lead Now", 201
Human Resource Skills for Project Managers, 9

I
"I" statements, 215
Iacocca, Lee, 205
implementation, 28
    consistency in project implementation, 38
influencing others, 170
innovation, 170
    encouraging, 173-176
    fueled by lessons learned, 75-76
    observing and questioning how things are done, 192-193
inspiration, 156-157
instrumental leadership, 156-157
    knowledge of experienced leaders, 158
integrity, demonstrating, 60, 154
interdependence in project environment, 154
    understanding the concept, 155
interesting work, ensuring, 228-229
internal customers, 106-107
interpersonal skills, 27
invincibility, feelings of, 2-3
Irwin, Eugene, 49
IT project managers, survey of, 89-90

J
Jackson, Angela, 211
jerk-dom, avoiding, 134

K
Kanter, Rosabeth Moss, 179
Katzenbach, Jon R., 201
"Keeping the Crisis in Chrysler", 1-3
keeping your back to the wall, 2
Kemp, Ron, 31
Kerzner, Harold, xiv, 7, 37, 66, 186
key performance indicators. *See* KPIs
keyboards, 173
kinetic, 159
kinetic energy, 160
knowledge bank of leadership, xix, 200
knowledge, new ideas from, 118
knowledge sharing, 11
Knutson, Joan, 124
Koestler, Arthur, 191
Kouzes, James, 153, 163
KPIs (key performance indicators), iv, 146
Kranz, Gene, 139, 194
Kroc, Ray, 204

L
The Last Castle, 49
The Last Lecture, 233-237
leaders
    definitions of, 49-50
    needing new leadership, 169-170
    project managers as, 9
leadership
    adaptive, 126-127
    assessing leadership qualities, 111-114, 194, 200
    business savvy and, 25
    common sense in, 180
    defined, iv, 10-11, 156-157
    difference between managing and leading, 44
    getting started, xvii-xviii
    increasing knowledge bank of leadership, xviii

instrumental leadership, 156
leading like everyone's watching, 59-61
leaders or leadership team in businesses, 25
lesson from *The Last Lecture*, 235-236
lessons from *Star Trek, The Next Generation*, 95-101
managing your leadership role, 139-142
of meetings, 19-22
Nine Cs of, 206-208
SWOT analysis, 12-15
Leadership (Giuliani), 50-51, 60
The Leadership Challenge, 157-158
leadership checklist, creating, 145-150
    asking questions on leaders and leadership, 146-147
    example checklist, 146-147
leadership formula, 199-200, 203
    statement of, 201-202
leadership lessons learned. *See* lessons learned
leadership reviews, 139, 141, 142
lessons learned, 73-77
    collection of, from experienced leaders, 76-77
    combining with new ideas, 118-119
    importance of documenting and sharing, 11
    from *The Last Lecture*, 235-236
    from *Star Trek, The Next Generation*, 97-101
Lewis, James P., 9, 27,
limitations, knowing, 141, 169
Lipman-Blumen, Jean, 155
line management leadership, x-xiv
listening, xviii, 154
    active listening, xvii
    in conflict resolution, 213
    in meetings, 21
Lombardi, Vince, xii, 65
luck versus preparedness, 124

M

MacArthur, Douglas, 60
Magnum Force (movie), 142, 169
Make It So – Leadership Lessons from Star Trek, The Next Generation, 97
management skills, 27, 169
management's expectations, 200
manager-subordinate relationships, xii
managers
    general managers and project managers, 29-31
    project managers as, xvii
"Managing Conflict", 211
managing versus leading, 44
Maxwell, John C., 2xix, 1, 7, 29, 49, 205
McDonald's, 201
meeting impeder, 20
meetings, leadership of, 19-22
    tips from meeting leaders, 19
mental locks, 119
mentors of leaders, 170
Merrill, Rebecca A., xiv
Merrill, Roger A., xiv
Microsoft ad, 173
Microsoft Windows Server ad, 199
millennials (generation X and Y employees), motivation of, 133
Miracle (movie), 140
mission
    project, 38
    propelled by effective leaders, 159
mistakes, capitalizing on, 176
motivation, 124, 156
    ability to motivate a team or organization, 163

compensation and monetary rewards, 133
dendrite stretchers, 152-153
understanding for team members, 132

N
Nader, Ralph, 173
Neal, Patricia, 219
negative behaviors and actions, focus on, 140
negative leadership, 49
"A New World Order", 105
Nightingale, Earl, 81
Nine Cs of Leadership, 205-208
nonverbal communications, 164

O
objectives, xiv, 220
    expectations versus, 222
    questions answered by, 222
    SMART, 220
observation, intense, practicing, 191-195
Ono, Dan, vii, 82
opportunities. *See also* SWOT analysis
    analyzing, 13-14
    finding in difficult situations, 175
optimistic words, 157
overconfidence, 1
oyakudachi (walking in the customer's shoes), 105-107

P
participatory leadership, 51
Pasteur, Louis, 125
Patton, George S., 60
Pausch, Randy, 234, 236
pay, motivation and, 133
peace phrases, developing, 214
people success, importance of

communication, xvii
personal skills, 28
Peters, Tom, 134, 142, 165, 166, 185
Pinto, Jeffrey K., 38
planning
    emphasis on, 39
    strategic and tactical, 28
planning, implementation, and evaluation (PIE), 74
PMI (Project Management Institute)
    Leadership in Project Management Annual-2005 Volume I, 186
    PMBOK® Guide, definition of leadership, 156
    PMBOK® Guide, 4th edition, 29
    PMNetwork magazine, 124
    Role Delineation Study, 11
    Seminar/Symposium, 233
positive attitude and presence, maintaining, 125, 134, 157
positive behaviors of team, focusing on, 139-140
positive leadership, xvi, 52, 153
    building, key factors in, 154
    final thoughts on, 239
positive thinking, 236
Posner, Barry, 153, 163
Powell, Colin, xix, 73
The Power of Acknowledgment, 7
power level, checking, 141
power of well-defined leadership, 156
pride, as key factor in success, 201
problem statement, 223
product-vendor evaluation, 28
"project away teams", 98
project environments
    characteristics of, xii
    interdependence in, 155
project leadership, xvi. *See also* leadership

defined, 11
future of, 46
redefining, 49-55
leading to succeed, 28
meetings, leadership of, 19-22
traditional, x-xii
project management
   future of, 46
   individuals contributing to value of, 233
   sources of information on, 233
   Project Management Institute. *See* PMI
"A Project Management Renaissance: The Future Is Already Here", 124
project management speak versus. executive speak, 187
Project Management: A Systems Approach to Planning, Scheduling, and Controlling, 10th edition, 67
project managers
   communications with executive levels, 92
   and general managers, 29-31
   important skills for, 27, 179
   roles of, 8-9
   twelve factors in, 38-49
project team
   creativity in, importance of, 117-120
   establishing roles for, 65-69
   explaining requirements to, 83
   high-performing, surrounding yourself with, 127
   leadership from within, 170
   retaining key members, 131-135
   spending time with, 141
project wow!ers, 164
   becoming, things you can do, 165-166
projects
   as financial investments, 26
   meetings as, 20
   promises, keeping, 133
   purpose, xv
   for meetings, 21
The Pursuit of Wow! Every Person's Guide to Topsy-Turvy Times, 165

Q

quality assurance, 29
quantitative failure, x
questioning how things are done, 192
questions, asking, 85

R

realistic words, 157
recharging the leader, 140
recognition pit stops, 22
recognition and reward for team members, 132
recognition, reward, and rest, on project closure, 2-4
Redford, Robert, 49
relational leadership, 156, 188
resiliency, 194
resource issues, 92
Retaining Your Best People, 132
retention of key team members, 131-135
   tips for, 134-135
risk situations, avoiding, 92-93
risks, becoming more aware of, 125
roadblocks to project startup, 89-90
Roberts, Wess, 97
roles
   establishing for project team, 65-69
   PMI Role Delineation Study, 11
   of project managers, 10
Room to Read, 180
Roosevelt, Franklin D., 173

root cause analysis, 223
Ross, Bill, 97
rules, questioning, 176

S

savvy. *See also* business savvy, project managers and
    definitions of, 25
schedules, unrealistic, 92
scope/quality, in triple constraint, 38
sense of direction, xv
September 11, 2001, terrorist attacks, 51, 73
The 7 Habits of Highly Effective People, 179
Shelton, Lee, 74
SMART objectives, 221
soft skills, 179
speaking leadership, 156
standards, procedures, and policies, 28
stand-up comedians, 193
Star Trek, The Next Generation, leadership lessons from, 97-101
Stevenson, Adlai, 110
strategic or innovative values, 37, 38
strategic leadership, 146-147
strategic planning, 28-29
    leadership checklist for, 146-147
strengths, weaknesses, opportunities, and threats. *See* SWOT analysis
success
    creating a vision, 4
    defining, 3
    definitions of, 35
    improving upon, 176
    innovation as essential ingredient, 176
    keeping your back to the wall, 2
    leading to succeed, 11
    measurements of, 4-5, 31 42
    remembering the driver, 3, 108
    and seeking further success, 2-3
superior-subordinate relationships, x
supervision, minimizing, 135
suppliers, 106
    customer-supplier model, 107
    selection and relationships with, 28
support
    from a distance, for virtual teams, 101
    visible, 39
supportive roles, project team members, 68
sustainable future, 38
SWOT (strengths, weaknesses, opportunities, and threats) analysis, 12-15
systems and technology integration, 28
systems thinking, 153

T

tactical planning, 29
"Talk Elevated", 186
team. *See* project team
technical skills, 90
technology
    creating even playing field in international arena, 74
    management of, x
    rapid pace of change in, 73
    systems and technology integration, 28
    systems thinking and, 155
templates and lists, 38
testing, 28
thinking outside the box, 194
Tough Minded Leadership, 10
threats. *See also* SWOT analysis
    analyzing, 13-14
time, in triple constraint, 26
traditional leadership, xii
transformational leadership, 155.

See also instrumental leadership
treating project team well, 201-202
triple constraint, 26, 28, 35
trust, 60, 154
typewriters, sticking keys problem, 174

U
Umlas, Judith W., ii, 7
urgency, sense of 141

V
value
    creating, factors of project leadership and, 38
    identifying work that adds value, 228
    success and, 38-35
value assessment, 181
Value Driven Project Management, 35
Verma, Vijay, 9, 11
virtual teams, 98, 99
visibility of project leader, 109, 110, 133-134
visible support, 39
vision
    creating, 59
    project vision and mission, 59
von Oech, Roger, 118, 174

W
walking in the customer's shoes (oyakudachi), 105-107
Warner, Fara, 1-3
Wattleton, Fay, 145
weaknesses. *See also* SWOT analysis
    analyzing, 14
A Whack on the Side of the Head, 118, 120, 174
"what if" questions, asking, 175, 193
Where Have All the Leaders Gone?, 205

Why Pride Matters More Than Money, 201
Wood, John, 180
words commonly used by leaders, characteristics of, 156
words and phrases that escalate conflict, 213
work environment, rapid changes in, 73
world business environment, 73
The World Class Project Manager, 27
World Trade Center, terrorist attacks on, 51, 75
Wow! leadership, 163-166
Wow! projects, 134, 141, 164
Wysocki, Robert, 27

About International Institute for Learning, Inc.

With a wholly-owned network of operating companies all over the world and clients in more than 150 countries, IIL is a global leader in training, consulting, coaching and mentoring, as well as customized course development. Our core competencies include: Project, Program and Portfolio Management; Business Analysis; Microsoft® Project and Project Server; Lean Six Sigma; PRINCE2®; ITIL® Agile; Leadership and Interpersonal Skills.

Using our proprietary Many Methods of Learning™ enables us to deliver innovative, effective and consistent training solutions through a variety of learning approaches (Virtual Classroom, Traditional Classroom, Simulation Training, Interactive On-Demand Training and a blended approach). A PMI® Charter Global Registered Education Provider, a member of PMI's Global Executive Council, an Accredited Training Organization (ATO) for Prince2, MSP, ITIL, MOP, Agile, and a Microsoft Partner (with a Microsoft Gold Project and Portfolio Management competency) and an IIBA® Endorsed Education Provider, IIL is the training solution partner of choice for many top global companies.

For more information on IIL services, please visit www.iil.com or email learning@iil.com.